The American Barbershop
A Closer Look at a Disappearing Place

The American Barbershop
A Closer Look at a Disappearing Place

by
Mic Hunter

Foreword by
Norman Rosenberg, Ph.D.,

Face to Face Books
Mount Horeb, Wisconsin
1996

Face to Face Books is a national imprint of Midwest Traditions, Inc., a nonprofit organization working to help preserve a sense of place and tradition in American life. Our publications provide encounters with everyday people with extraordinary riches: their stories, their arts, their folkways, their lives.

The poem "Barbers" (on page 39) from *Something Permanent*, ©1994 by Cynthia Rylant, is reprinted in its entirety by permission of Harcourt Brace & Company.

All other material quoted from various sources for interpretive purposes is gratefully acknowledged.

Book Design: MacLean & Tuminelly
Editor: Philip Martin

For a catalog of books and other materials, write:
Face to Face Books/Midwest Traditions
P.O. Box 320
Mount Horeb, Wisconsin 53572 U.S.A.
or call 1-800-736-9189.

Library of Congress Cataloging-in-Publication Data
Hunter, Mic.
    The American barbershop : a closer look at a disappearing place / by Mic Hunter : foreword by Norman Rosenberg.—1st ed.
        p.   cm.
    Includes bibliographical references.
    ISBN 1-883953-14-6 (pbk.)
    1. Barbershops—United States—History.   2. Barbershops—United States—History—Pictorial works.   3. Barbering—United States—History.   4. Barbering—United States—History—Pictorial works.   I. Title.
TT957.H87   1996
646.7'24'0973—dc20   96-6018
                                                                           CIP

First Edition
10 9 8 7 6 5 4 3 2 1

This book is dedicated to the photographers of *Life* and *National Geographic*
for what they gave my eyes when I was a boy in a small town,
and to my nephew, David Brown, a remarkable boy
who will grow into a splendid man.

This book is made possible
in part with the kind support of
the William Marvy Company
of St. Paul, Minnesota,
the nation's premiere maker of barber poles since 1950
founded by the late William Marvy
1909–1993

Babies haven't any hair;
Old men's heads are just as bare;
Between the cradle and the grave
Lies a haircut and a shave.
—*Samuel Hoffenstein (1890–1947)*

Table of Contents

List of Tables

Foreword

A recent television commercial portrays a young man plugging dandruff shampoo. At the beginning of the piece, when he refers to the young woman fussing with his hair as "his barber," she quickly corrects him. She is a "stylist." At the end of the commercial, he starts to use the "b-word" again; but now, before the word escapes his lips, he corrects himself. An important cultural divide, it seems, has been crossed.

Although Mic Hunter's *The American Barbershop* was begun before this commercial was even conceived, his insightful book explores the complex culturescape that animates this deceivingly simple television narrative. Barbering and hairstyling—Madison Avenue and *The American Barbershop* both recognize this, albeit in their own ways—are very different practices that offer very different meanings to customers, to practitioners, and to the culture at large.

In short, Mic Hunter's celebration of the traditional barbershop deftly goes beyond a merely celebratory or nostalgic account. It is a multi-layered, hybrid work: a photo essay, a social and cultural history, a personal reminiscence, and (appropriate to Hunter's professional concerns) a psychologically informed ethnography.

The American Barbershop thus joins a growing number of historically oriented studies that look back not simply at "time" but also at "place." It was in special places such as the school room, the factory floor, the front porch, the backyard—and the barber (and beauty) shop—that cultural practices and values were transferred, and transformed, across generations.

This book encouraged me to reflect on a very special place to my own times: a one-chair shop in which a Holocaust survivor blended the barbering rituals of pre-Nazi Poland to those of the American Middle West. Where else in Lincoln, Nebraska, could a young boy learn Yiddish slang while simultaneously perusing the latest popular comic books?

I am confident that even those who are using Mic Hunter's wonderful book to enter the traditional barbershop for the first time will find themselves reflecting on the multi-layered, and highly gendered, meanings of a unique, and perhaps endangered, place in American life.

—Dr. Norm Rosenberg
  DeWitt Wallace Professor of History
  Macalester College
  August 1995

Preface

"But Is It Art?"

yes you can make a buck
selling hairdos
but is it art?
I had a fellow in
once a week
who used to have himself
photographed
at the studio
down the street
every time
I cut his hair
he said he figured those photos
would mean something someday
to somebody
yeah when the world
rediscovers the ordinary....
—David Beaver (1984)

Over the years I have been asked hundreds of times my motivation for doing this project. Every time I entered a barbershop and asked permission to make photographs, everyone wanted to know, "What are you going to do with the pictures? Who is paying you to do this? Who cares about pictures of an old barbershop?" When I told them I wanted to capture on film something important that is disappearing, the customers laughed and exclaimed, "What are you talking about? There will always be barbershops!" But the barbers would stop what they were doing and quietly say, "No, he's right. We can't compete. Someday we will all be gone."

Once my reason for being there was known, everyone was cooperative and had an opinion on the fate of barbershops. When one barber learned that I make my living not as a photographer but as a psychotherapist, he said that explained my interest in barbers. He observed, "We are in the same line of work. We both get paid to listen to people's problems. I carry other people's pain the same way you do,

son. I just also give them a haircut to remember me by."

Many of the barbers were moved that I would spend my personal funds and time to document their profession. More than once, as I was about to leave a shop after having spent an afternoon talking and making photographs, the barber would ask me to stop. He would slowly open a drawer, remove something, and come over to me. He would place an old, but well-maintained straight razor in my hand. I would examine it for the treasure it was as he said, "That was my father's when he was a barber. He gave it to me when I graduated from barber college." As I would attempt to return it to him, he would press it into my hand. "No. You take it. I don't have any use for it. Nobody asks for a shave anymore." I would protest, "Don't you want to pass it on to one of your children? Your son?" Again, he would take my hand and gently lay the razor in my palm. "No, he doesn't understand the way you do. I want you to have it. You'll take care of it." These razors are mounted on my bathroom wall—gifts from men I knew for only a few hours and will never see again. I hope this book honors their memory as I intended.

This project is not and was never meant to be a thorough scholarly examination of the historical, political, social, and psychological aspects of barbering. I merely set out to document the vanishing of an important component of my childhood. I have been fascinated by photographing humans ever since, while in Mr. Jeskey's seventh grade photography club, I stomped on my mother's foot to photograph her reaction. I still have this photograph. I doubt that my mother has yet forgiven me for my excessive use of artistic license at her expense.

These photographs were done in my spare time from 1982 through 1996. I used both 35mm and 120mm cameras. When traveling on business, I took a 35mm camera with a 28mm to 85mm zoom lens. When I had my medium-format camera with me, I used the waist-level viewfinder so that I could maintain eye contact with the subjects. The film was exposed at speeds between 400 and 6400 ASA. I learned early on that a flash does not mix well with the reflective surfaces and mirrors of a barbershop. None of the photographs were posed. They are all spontaneous moments of time frozen as I witnessed them.

After photographing in more than half of the states in the country, I began to see as the theme of this project the common characteristics that many barbershops share. In general, locations of shops and names of barbers are not given in the text. Some of the shops have closed, or the barbers retired since I took these photographs, and I chose in most cases to keep names of those who confided in me and shared details of their lives anonymous. Do not assume that the stories in a chapter come from the individuals or barbershops appearing in the photographs in that section. If so inspired, I strongly encourage you to visit your own local barbershop, where you will hear many of the same stories that I did.

I will take this opportunity to thank the people who helped me complete this project: the staffs of the St. Paul Public Library, the Roseville Public Library, the Minnesota Historical Society Library, and Terri Fischell at the Macalester College Library, all of whom helped me find my research materials; the staff of the Virginia (Minnesota) Public Library who left me alone as a child to devour every photography book in their collection; Norm Rosenberg who captured my attention as an undergraduate student when I had planned only on fulfilling the school's liberal-arts requirement by taking a single history class, but ended up earning a minor in American history; Norma Hunter who encouraged me when I wanted to join the Seventh Grade Photography Club; Bob Marvy for taking time out of his busy day to meet with me; Bob Lewis, Marion Stafford and David Wilks who went out of their way to see that I gained access to a certain barbershop which had been boarded up; Edwin C. Jeffers for his rapid response to my request for information from the Barber Museum; Teresa and Cory at the Prairie Star Coffee House for agreeing to display my photos; and Phil Martin whose friendly warm voice on the phone said that most wonderful of phrases, "Yes, I think it would make a great book."

The person who has earned the greatest amount of gratitude from me is Kate An Greenbaum Hunter. She graciously endured years of me slamming on our automobile's brakes every time we came within sight of a barbershop so I could get "just a couple of shots" before we again set out for wherever we were originally headed. She has believed in this project for as long as I have. She is the only person in all these years that did not ask me why I was spending my time and money photographing barbers. I do not know if I would have completed this task without her support.

Finally, I must thank all the barbers and their customers who let me into their shops and sometimes into their hearts.

I set out to document a vanishing childhood memory. I ended up with a celebration of the culture of today's barbers and their shops. I hope you share my joy in rediscovering this vibrant, richly-diverse place: the neighborhood barbershop just around the corner!

CHAPTER ONE

The Search for the Traditional Shop

A community life exists when one can go daily to a given location at a given time and see many of the people one knows.
—*Philip Slater (1971)*

... when the good citizens of a community find places to spend pleasurable hours with one another for no specific or obvious purpose, there is purpose to such association.
—*Ray Oldenburg (1989)*

As sociologist Ray Oldenburg points out in his 1989 book, *The Great Good Place*, all great cultures have had a vitally rich informal public life, anchored by gathering spots where people meet outside of work or home, often by chance. The barbershop is one such gathering spot especially for men. With its familiar sweet smells, soothing snip of scissors and hum of electric razors, relaxed schedule, and idle banter, this masculine environment holds a special significance for about one-half of the American population.

Unfortunately, during the latter part of the 20th century, these neighborhood-based haircutting places have been slowly but steadily dwindling in number, and in familiarity for too many of us. Perhaps we should take a closer look at the barbershop for our own good, before it is too late. Of course, as long as there are people with hair, there will be establishments where hair can be cut or otherwise manipulated. Yes, there will always be haircare emporiums—but there may not always be barbershops. At least not what I mean by a barbershop.

This is unfortunate. With the closing of each barbershop we lose something important, in the same way that each time a supermarket replaces a Mom and Pop grocery, or a fast-food franchise puts a local drive-in burger joint out of business, we suffer a loss, a disappearance of individuality. Perhaps America is a great melting pot, but variety is the spice of life. The more I travel, the fewer reasons I see to travel. America's streets are lined with chainstores, each town becoming a carbon copy of the last. I have heard now there is even a franchise of the bar which was the set for the television program, *Cheers*. I find this ironic: to imitate a television setting for a neighborhood saloon, whose theme song lyrics described as a place "where everybody knows your name." The appeal of the saloon was a unique place where people were known as individuals. So someone comes up with the idea of packaging the familiarity, building identical "unique bars" throughout the country.

Barbershops have been affected by this trend for some time. The Bureau of the Census reported that between 1972 and 1977, the number of barbershops declined 25%. That is a very big drop in five years. Once gone, these neighborhood establishments are unlikely to return. This saddens me. I think the one- or two-man barbershop is a special place—a place worth keeping as a part of our society.

The barbershops I visited I have labeled as *traditional*. The term does not mean obsolete or even old. There are traditional shops that have recently been built. When I asked one of the barbers I was photographing if there were any other traditional shops nearby, he responded, "If by *tradi-tional*, you mean a penny gumball machine in the corner and a dead animal head mounted on the wall—then there's only one besides mine."

I used to ask the bell captains at hotels where I stayed for directions to the nearest barbershop. But I soon learned this method led to many dead ends. Without realizing it, young bell captain were likely to tell me where a barbershop *used* to be. They would recall having seen a shop at some time, but since they did not get their hair cut there, they did not notice when the shop closed. I also tried using the *Yellow Pages*. I would look under "Barbers." Unfortunately, phonebook ads did not distinguish well between a unisex hair salon and a traditional barbershop.

To further add to the difficulty, some barbershops do not have phones, and so are not listed in the directory. As one barber told me, "I been cuttin' here the same times of the week for twenty-seven years. What does anybody need to call me for? I don't take appointments. I don't need a phone or business cards. If a guy doesn't know where I am after twenty-seven years, he ain't likely to come looking for me during the next twenty-seven."

I found the best technique was to go to the police station, and ask the desk sergeant where the nearest traditional barbershop was located. Needing a bit of clarification, one officer asked, "By *traditional* shop, do you mean *regular* shop?"

Webster's Dictionary defines the word *tradition* as "the delivery of opinions, doctrines, practices, rites, and customs from generation to generation by oral communication."

That sort of sums up the barbershop, doesn't it? Some believe that tradition stifles people and prevents growth. That would be true of *rigid* tradition—but tradition need not be inflexible. More importantly, a society which ignores its tradition is like a boat without a rudder; it will get someplace but it's hard to predict where that place will be.

Once I found the first barbershop, the rest were easy to find. I would merely ask the first barber where the other traditional shops were located. To my amazement, in most cases he not only knew the names of other barbers and the addresses of their shops, but he also knew how long they had been in business—and sometimes where their previous shops had been located.

Of course, there is a difference between barbershops and hairstyling salons or beauty parlors. A barbershop is a place to maintain grooming (to "groom" is to cause to be tidy or neat). Beauty shops and hairstyling salons, however, are in the business of creating beauty or style– higher ideals than mere neatness.

Accordingly, the styles in which shops are decorated are different. Beauty salons are designed to look glamorous, while hairstylists are modern—and their shop fixtures and decorations reflect this. Barbershops, however, are supposed to be comfortable. It is common to see nearly every inch of the walls of a barbershop covered with various objects, a style that one barber labeled "early exploding Salvation Army."

One obvious clue to tell if you are in a beauty salon or hairstylist's shop, or in a barbershop, is if there is a tanning bed. Men who go to barbershops do not pay to lie around under artificial sunlight. They get their tans naturally, a by-product of working and playing out of doors.

Beyond the fixtures or the "look" of the place, the use of language clearly reflects a difference in basic attitude. Barbers have *customers*. Hair salons have *clients*. Furthermore, notice that in the term *barbershop*, the focus is on a person: the barber. The focus of a *hairstyling salon* is on the product: the hairstyle.

This same difference can be seen in how the business is named. Barbershops are commonly named for the barber who owns them. On the contrary, hairstyling salons have names designed to make a statement or create an image. To illustrate, let's look at the business section of the phone book from the northern Minnesota town of Brainerd, with a population of 12,500 in 1991. Under the heading "Barbers," I found sixteen businesses listed. However, when I double-checked to see if some of those names were also listed under the heading "Beauty Salons," I weeded out nine of the shops as unisex salons, leaving only seven that were actually traditional barbershops (Table 1, overleaf).

As you can see, each traditional shop was named for its owner-operator, the barber. In sharp contrast, the hair salons had fashionable, fanciful names, often involving a play on words.

Table 1
Shops listed in the telephone book under "Barbers" and "Beauty Salons" in Brainerd, Minnesota.

Shops listed in phone book only under "Barbers"	Shops listed in phone book under "Beauty Salons"
Duane's	Beauty Haven*
Jim's	City Looks*
Johnson's	Cut Above
Murph's	Fashion Flair*
Spike's	Golden Touch Coiffures*
Tuck's	Hair Affair
Vern's	Hair Company*
	Hair N Things*
	Hair Village
	Nu-look Unlimited*
	Paragon Hair Design*
	Shear Joy*
	Stylists Chateau

* These shops cross-listed in the phone book under both "Beauty Salons" *and* "Barbers."

Something that has always puzzled me: why, although females make up 51% of the general population, do they require so many beauty salons? For example, in St. Paul, Minnesota, with a population of 272,000 people, the business section of the phonebook lists 421 beauty salons—one for every 329.5 females. On the other hand, there are only 89 barbershops and 53 unisex hairstyling shops. That means 938.6 men for every shop. No wonder I have to wait in line every time I want my hair cut.

This is not just a phenomenon of the Midwest. In 1992, the Board of Cosmetology & Hairstyling in Newark, New Jersey, counted a total of 64,725 beauticians and 9,630 hairstylists in the "Liberty and Prosperity State," but only 6,406 barbers! For a population of about 7.7 million, that means that even if all hairstylists cut only men's hair, there would still be 235 men for every barber and hairstylist, while each beautician would have only 60 women to attend to.

During my travels, I met several barbers who had previously been employed in hair salons. Their stories were similar to the story of the man who told me the following:

> When I graduated from barber school I didn't want to be like my old man and work in an old-fashioned shop, so I moved to the city and got a job cutting hair in a fancy shop where I had to wear a vest and a tie. I couldn't stand it. Everything seemed so phony. I kept it up till I thought I would scream. I finally couldn't stand it anymore. When I was on the phone with my dad I told him that I was going to quit the trade and learn to do something else.

He didn't try to argue me out of it, but he suddenly just happened to decide to go on a two-week vacation— longer than he had ever taken before—and asked me if I would look after his shop till he got back. I agreed.

> That was 20 years ago. He gave me the opportunity to see that the reason I was unhappy in that fancy shop wasn't because I didn't like cutting hair, it was that I didn't like kissin' people's butts. I stayed in his shop when he came back from vacation and finally took it over when he died. I followed his policy, "If it's a pain in the butt to cut a certain guy's hair, just tell him to go to another shop. Life's too short to spend your time with those kind of people." I feel sorry for guys who don't enjoy their work.

Barbershops are stable, steady businesses, good for a neighborhood. They provide a steady stream of potential customers for other nearby businesses. Many barbers do not even have business cards. Those who do often do not bother to have their zip code, or sometimes even their city, printed on them. Instead, the card may have a map or simple directions to the shop.

After visiting barbers for several years, I began to realize just how long they remained at one site. This is very different from my own work history; I changed location every five years. I eventually learned, if I asked a barber how long he had been in this shop and he replied something like, "Thirteen years," to say, "Well then, where was your shop before you relocated here?" This always won me a smile. Many small businesses today would brag about being at the same

location for thirteen years, but in barbershop time, that only made him the "new kid on the block."

Barbers are proud of their longevity. When I asked, "How long has the shop been here?" often I heard something like, "We've been here so long we gave a haircut to the busboy at the Last Supper!"

In barbershops, time is often measured not in years but in decades. This was true of one shop I visited where every twenty years a new barber had joined the shop. The former owner, now retired, was 80 years old. Each day, he came in when he felt like it, and worked on one or two customers, old-timers he had known forever. He was in the shop by choice. He came to be social, to be around other people—to be in a place he was known and respected. The other barbers still asked for his opinion and often prompted him to tell a cherished story or joke. "This isn't my office anymore, son, it's my living room!" he said with a laugh.

Next to his chair was the current owner's chair. At 60 years of age, he had "a few thousand haircuts still in me before I put the scissors down for good." He had started out at the shop as an apprentice. The deal was made—and sealed with a handshake—that if he worked out, showed up on time, didn't use curse words in front of customers, laughed at their jokes, avoided "railroading" or "soldiering," and didn't come in smelling of liquor, he'd be first in line to buy the shop from the old man.

Railroading, by the way, is hurrying the services of one customer in order get a waiting customer—especially if the one waiting was known as a big spender in the chair. *Soldier-*

ing is the opposite: working slowly on a customer to avoid having to serve an undesirable customer who is waiting for a chair to open up.

That trial period was completed many years ago, and now the name of the one-time apprentice was painted in red letters on the front window. But out of respect for the "old man," the phone was answered, not with the shop's new name, but merely, "Barbershop."

Moving on down the line, I met "the new barber." Aged 40, he was the "new kid." He had been there only two decades. He said he and the others always had their eyes open, looking for some 20-year-old to join the group. "That'll attract the younger generation who don't believe we can cut the new styles." He said he wanted to get someone in who had just finished barber school, but had not had time to develop any bad habits. "Better to train 'em yourself than to try to fix 'em, to get 'em to do it your way."

In this shop, it was plain to see that customers were waiting for their favorite barber's chair to open up. Was their motivation to wait due to the skill of a given barber—or their favorite topics of conversation? Was it force of habit, or outright loyalty?

Whatever the cause, the barbers never made the social error of inviting someone else's customer into their chair. Each merely stood aside his chair, looking out the window, until someone decided to plop down on the leather-covered seat. With a flurry of white, the haircloth would come floating down over the customer like new fallen snow. This was followed by the gentle tugging of tissue about the neck, to be

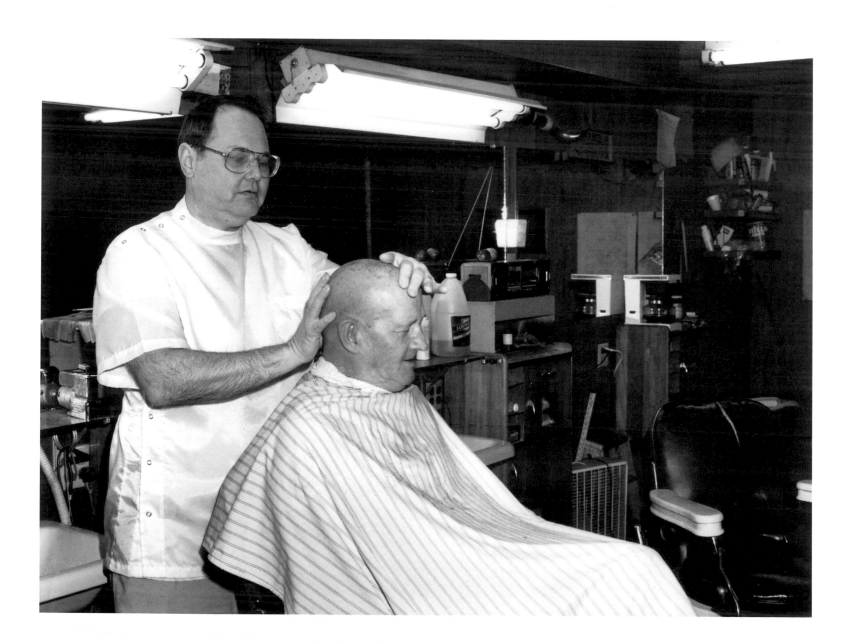

secured at the back by a clip cool to the skin. And then the opening question, "So … what will it be today?"

As if these barbers did not know the answer after all these years. The art in the barbering trade is to listen carefully to what the customer says he wants—and then give him enough of that so he is satisfied but still looks good. A barber is trained in what Charles De Zemler (1939) called the "fundamentals of face-design." Since faces and heads differ in size and shape, the same hairstyle looks different on each man. Therefore, the barber's task is to give the customer what he needs while making him believe he got what he wanted.

The response to the barber's opening question was fairly routine. "The usual," or "Same as last time." Sometimes there was a joke, "I was thinking I'd show up at church with a purple Mohawk. How do you think the choir would like that?" As the laughter died down, the barber would begin the task of producing "the usual,"—or "the same as last time," "short on the sides and long on top," "take some off—but not too much," "just enough so it doesn't stick up," "maybe a little longer for the cold months," or perhaps "a wee bit shorter now that it's hot." Never did the barber need to be reminded to include a scalp massage or give a once-over on the neck and shoulders with the noisy vibrator strapped on his hand.

The oldest practicing barber that I personally came across during my travels was 85 years old. He had been cutting hair at the same shop for 65 years. The day I met him, he was trimming the hair of a 60-year-old. The customer proudly noted that he had gotten his first haircut—and every haircut since—from this very barber. The customer insisted that the barber should stop smoking and take better care of his health, exclaiming, "Don't you up and die on me. At my age I'm too old to get used to a new barber."

There are a few barbers even more seasoned, if one looks in the right places. For example, E.R. "Bird" Harris in Reno is the oldest practicing barber in Texas (Flick, 1995). "Bird" Harris started cutting hair in 1926 and got around to getting a license four years later. At 91 years of age, he states that his success as a barber comes from doing one thing, and doing it well. In his shop, the customer knows exactly what he is going to get—as Mr. Harris offers only one style of haircut. "If a customer wants his hair cut some other way, he has to go to another barber," he explained.

The only other thing Mr. Harris requires of his customers is that they listen to his opinions. One long-time customer noted, "He charges only a little for the actual haircut, the rest of the fee is for his opinions." Mr. Harris's license was due to expire in 1995. But he assured everyone concerned that he planned to renew it, and had no plans to retire in the foreseeable future.

Although most shops measure the passing of years in decades, one shop measured time by lifetimes. This shop was haunted. The building had been a barbershop since it was built over 100 years ago. The current barber believed the spirit of one of the previous barbers still inhabited the shop. He sited evidence such as the phone ringing—even when he did not have phone service, or all the lights in the shop coming on suddenly, or things falling off the wall without any reasonable explanation.

Whenever any of this occurred, the owner figured the ghost was telling him it was time to close the shop for the day and go fishing or play golf. Perhaps the ghost barber had worked himself to death in the shop, and was just looking out for the most recent barber's well-being, chasing him out to play and relax once in awhile.

Still offering sound advice from the grave. Quite the barber.

CHAPTER TWO

The Ways of the Shop

"So ... what'll it be today?"
—*barber*

"Oh, same as usual."
—*customer*

Traditional barbershops and other public gathering places are the backbone of democracy. Some people fear that hanging out in such places leads to deviant behavior. Quite the opposite is more likely. When one is an accepted member of a group—even an informal group—one uses a mental image of the other members as a conscience. As Ray Oldenburg (1989) noted, a person is less likely to do something anti social if he eventually has to face his peers in the barbershop or other setting where his behavior will become the topic of conversation.

The barber is the link between the blue-collar laborer and the white-collar worker. Regardless of what you do with your hands, when you are in a barbershop you can be just another man—a regular guy. When former-President Richard Nixon died, who did the press seek out to discover the "real Dick Nixon?" A statesman? Another man who had held the same office? A scholar? A biographer? No, it was his barber—the man who cut his hair every week, year after year. Much to his credit, the barber had the courtesy to merely disclose,

"Mr. Nixon was a good tipper."

By the way, some of the barbers I talked with viewed themselves as specially trained, licensed service providers, and claimed that, unlike hairstylists, they did not accept tips. In fact, they said they would be insulted if a tip was offered. As one barber told me, "You would not think of offering a tip to your child's school teacher. Licensed professionals charge a fair price for their services. They are not to be tipped. It is only appropriate to tip untrained workers."

However, when I told one barber that I had met other barbers who claimed not to accept tips, he laughed and informed me that they were saying that so they wouldn't have to report the extra income to the Internal Revenue Service. This same man gave me some advice on the psychology of pricing:

> Have your posted price for a haircut be an uneven amount of money. That way the customer can easily say, 'Keep the change,' after he hands you a bill. That simple act will make the customer feel important and generous. It's much better to charge $6.50 and get a 50¢ tip, than to charge $7 for a haircut. Either way you get seven bucks for your work, but my way you also get a happy customer, and that is worth more than you can imagine.

One barber told me that people came to his shop because they liked the rules. There were only six rules, but they were strictly enforced:

1. No spitting on the floor.
2. No breaking the furniture.
3. No last names.
4. You wait your turn no matter how much money you make or how much education you have.
5. You wait your turn no matter who you are or how important you think you are.
6. Anything else goes.

A barber, Burr Cheever of Edina, Minnesota, had a customer who had first been brought by his father into Mr. Cheever's shop at age two, for the young lad's very first haircut. Subsequently, Mr. Cheever had trimmed this same head of hair every month for 62 years thereafter. When asked the name of this regular customer, the barber's reply was, "I don't know. He never told me and I never asked." For six decades, Mr. Cheever's philosophy had been, "As long as the fella pays for his haircut, he shouldn't have to worry about inquisitive barbers" (Klobuchar, 1988).

Likely Mr. Cheever would agree with Morris Germano, proprietor of the Androy Barber Shop, who had sixteen rules and regulations for successful barbering posted in his shop. Among them was: "No loud talking allowed, answer your customer when spoken to, but don't start a conversation, relating your life's history, and above everything, don't argue with anybody" (*Krank's Review*, July 1929). This tradition of the quiet barber came to America from England, where the story was told of the barber who asked a well-known statesman, "How shall I cut your beard, my lord?" His lordship replied, "In silence" (J.B.H.C., 1934).

Still, easy-going conversation is generally considered part of the ambience of the barbershop. Although barbers hear many things from their customers, not all of what they hear is truthful. The barber in the town of Dime Box, Texas, claimed that barbers are the third most lied-to people in the world. He noted that the only people who hear more lies than barbers are wives and priests (Least Heat Moon, 1982).

Barbers have always been in the public eye. Therefore, they have to watch how they behave. In 1931, the Association of Master Barbers of America reminded its members: "The responsibility of reputation—a great responsibility rests upon the man with a laudable reputation. You cannot LIVE ON the reputation of a successful barber business, but must continually strive to LIVE UP to it."

Moses Jenkins, of the Champion Barber Shop in Harlem, carries on this tradition. He sees the barber as a role model for the community. He says, "Barber's got to live as careful a life as a minister. Just like these athletes, a lot is expected out of certain people. And a barber falls into that category. A barber can't be jumping up and down doing anything he wants to do just any kind of way. Barbering's just like a church. Everyone from a drunkard to the pastor comes in" (Blount, 1986).

A barber is many things to his customer. He is political commentator; he is sports and news reporter. He hears confessions. He gives advice. For some he is the father they never had, or a reminder of the father that has passed on. The touch a man receives at the barbershop may be the only physical contact, other than a handshake, that he will ever experience from another man. If the customer is a widower, it may be the only touch he receives anymore from anyone.

Norman Wasserman (1988) compared his relationship with his barbers to his relationships with his lovers. He stated that in both of these relationships he got the "seven-month itch" to try out a new one. He wrote, "As a rule of thumb a man has as many barbers in his lifetime as he has affairs. They include one-cut visits as well as liaisons that go on for years."

However, I have been struck by the loyalty customers have for their barbers. I once witnessed a man wait three hours in a multi-chair shop so he could get his hair cut by his favorite barber. Barber Walter Okane told me, "I've moved three times in 30 years. I still have customers that started with me in my first shop. I've got a guy who comes from Duluth [140 miles away] to get his hair cut. Nowadays only us old dogs know how to cut a flat-top."

One customer advised me as he rose from the barber's chair, "This guy gives the best damn haircut in the world, and I should know—I've been around the world eleven times." The customer was the captain of an ocean-going ship. When he was in port, he came in for his annual haircut. In between, he refused to let any other barber touch him.

Some barbers are equally devoted to their customers. I saw a barber plan the dates of his vacation so that a man, a long-time customer, could continue to come in for his twice-a-month haircut on the usual days. The barber told me that this fellow had been so regular that, if the customer ever did not show up on an expected day, the police would get a call

asking them to check the fellow's home to see if he had fallen or was ill.

In his 1989 book, *The Great Good Place*, Ray Oldenburg suggests that everyone needs three places in which to fully live their lives:

1. a place to live and be with family (a home),
2. a site to be productive (a work place), and
3. a gathering place (a home away from home), that Oldenburg calls the "Third Place."

The "Third Place" provides relief from the stresses and duties associated with the first two places. Oldenburg is concerned that America does not provide enough of these sanctuaries for voluntary human contact. After all, humans are social animals. If we do not get enough of the right types of human contact, we start acting goofy. Perhaps for that reason, the three best-selling drugs in America have been Tagamet, Inderal, and Valium treating and tranquilizing the symptoms of ulcers, hypertension (high blood pressure), and anxiety (Wallis, 1983). In his book, Oldenburg identified characteristics of his so-called Third Places:

They are easily accessible. Barbershops are easy to identify, often by a barber pole clearly visible from the street. The front wall often consists of plate glass, so you can easily see who is inside.

They maintain a low profile. Although easily found, barbershops and other Third Places are usually simple in appearance. When the poet Ralph Waldo Emerson wrote that there are no temples to friendship, he may have been thinking of barbershops. A temple is defined in the dictionary as "a building, usually large or pretentious, devoted to some public use." Barbershops are public, but anything but pretentious. They are often plain, never elegant, as if they are purposely attempting to be unimpressive.

Oldenburg suggests that perhaps the tendency to be a wee bit on the seedy side might serve to keep one-time visitors or women from wandering in and disrupting the "regulars." He also noted that since the surroundings are plain, customers are free to come as they are, and do not experience any pressure to dress up. This lack of pretense helps level out the effects of social class, so that everyone can relax.

Attendance is not mandatory. Part of the accessibility of a Third Place is the loose timing. You are free to come and go as you wish. Appointments are not made. Visits vary in length depending on one's mood.

The activities are spontaneous and unplanned. You never know who is going to be present—or when they will arrive, or how long they will stay. The activities depend on who shows up and what kind of mood they are experiencing. One day, a visitor may find himself in the middle of a heated debate on a serious topic, only to find the next time that the mood has changed to telling light-hearted stories. You can never predict exactly what is going to happen; this is part of the appeal of the place.

They are stable. Although this may seem to contradict the idea that Third Places are spontaneous and unplanned, places like barbershops are also stable. For example, the appearance—furnishings and decorations—remain the same

year after year. Rather than seeing change as improvement, most customers dread any alteration in their barber's shop. They do not mind if the shop is not painted with the latest fad color. More than once, when I witnessed a barber attempt to make a change in his shop, he was met with cries of protest. "I must be paying you too much if you've got money to waste on remodeling." "What was wrong with the old way?"

They are inclusive. Many organizations require membership of some type, or formal criteria which excludes some persons. Barbershops and other Third Places tend to be inclusive, places where people from all backgrounds can gather and enjoy the company of others with whom they may not otherwise associate.

In such places, acceptance of newcomers, although not automatic, is fairly easy. All a newcomer needs to show is that he is capable of decent conversation, and is not obnoxious. I have spent hours in barbershops during my very first, and only, visit, and have been treated as if I had been "a regular" for years.

Conversation is the primary activity. Just as one may go to a saloon to have a glass of beer, even if the refrigerator at home is full of bottles, men sometimes go to a barbershop even if they do not need a haircut. And they may stick around long after their hair has been trimmed, just to enjoy the company of other men.

In my travels, I noticed that many barbershops had two entrances: a front door for customers coming primarily to get their hair cut, and a back door for men coming mostly for companionship. Near each door was a group of chairs. Everyone seemed to understand the system. When a barber's chair emptied, someone from the front of the room filled it, while the guys in back stayed put. No explanation was needed.

The talk in Third Places is lively, colorful, and engaging. There is frequent laughter, dramatic story-telling, and back slapping. The American writer William Least Heat Moon (1982) must have been hanging out in the wrong shops when he wrote:

> If you want to hear distortions and misconceptions laced with plenty of dogmatic opinion, you have a choice of three places—excluding domed governmental edifices and buildings with steeples—bars, sport arenas, and gas stations (barbershops have lost position because you can't hear over the hair dryers).

Well, none of the barbershops I visited had any hair dryers that drowned out the conversation. If anything, the conversation overwhelmed the sound of any machinery—be it hair dryer, clippers, fan, or television.

Clearly, Third Places draw you into becoming an active participant, rather than an observer. And what is it that captures your attention? The conversation, of course! As Oldenburg put it:

> In third places, the agenda of conversation is not dominated by the mundane matters of home maintenance,

32

children's braces, who's going to take one child here and the other one there, and the like, nor by that tether that repeatedly brings workplace talk back to the office or shop. Novelty in third place conversation is lent by the predictable changes but unpredictable direction that it always takes. What trivia will be dredged up from the past and what outlandish speculations made about the future? Who will drag in a tidbit of gossip and how reliable and how spicy will it be? What cases shall this court of universal appeals try on any given day and what judgments shall its judges render? Will the tone be argumentative or agreeable? Will one nod in sympathetic accord or stare incredulously at the author of some asinine pronouncement? Will one be amused, challenged, or merely reinforced in one's prejudices? All of these, certainly.

The mood is playful. Although serious topics get discussed in barbershops, a witty remark is never long off. Nothing—death, sex, religion, the government—is so sacred it cannot be the focus of a joke. Georg Simmel (1971) suggested that quality human social interaction can be described in three words: joy, relief, and vivacity (i.e. "lively or animated"). Such interactions bring forth well-being. They offer a break from monotony and recharge one's emotional reserves. It has been estimated that, on average, an American laughs approximately fifteen times *a day* (Feinsilber and Mead, 1980). However, those who hang out in Third Places are more likely to laugh fifteen times *per hour* (Oldenburg, 1989). No wonder people are drawn to spend time in such places.

There is warmth. The playfulness extends not only to topics being discussed but to the customers as well. No man who expects to be a regular can take himself too seriously, because no person who is a familiar member of the group will be excluded from a little good-natured ridicule. In a barbershop, you do not have to wonder if you are liked if they make fun of you. However, if they are too polite and don't give you a hard time, then you know you have not yet been accepted into the group. When a man enters a barbershop, he is likely to be greeted not only by the barber but other customers as well. Each time the door opens, it is an occasion to stop and acknowledge the new addition to the group.

A barbershop is a place for men. It is important to understand that periodically separating the sexes in this way does not necessarily lead to sexism. Males (and females) need a place where they can be alone with their own gender. In America, the barbershop (and the beauty parlor) have traditionally been places where such bonding could take place. You may have noticed how often a barbershop and a beauty parlor exist near one another, yet maintain a distinct separateness.

Having a place like this for men can definitely lead to a greater acceptance of one's own gender. In turn, this can help increase appreciation of the other gender. In fact, a marriage that includes a broad support system has a better chance of surviving than one that relies solely on the wife and husband (Oldenburg, 1989).

So when are we going to see women's magazines featuring articles with titles like: "How to Get Your Husband to Spend More Time at the Barbershop?"

American men have been taught that they must remain "real men" in the presence of any female. Maintaining such a front requires effort. For many men, the only time they can truly relax is when they are in the presence only of other men.

Other societies have recognized the importance of men being with men. Many cultures in Asia, Africa, the Pacific Islands, Europe, and the Americas had a men's house in the village—a gathering place for the men. Only after completing a rite of passage were boys allowed to enter the men's house. There, boys learned the role and skills of manhood (Hutton, 1968).

Males have too few opportunities to bond in friendship and to learn what it means to be a man from one another. I know this because I make my living providing psychotherapy for men who are hungry to understand themselves and their masculinity. Frequently, the places they have turned for instruction in manhood have not been helpful. Too many rituals of masculinity in this society involve a risk of injury or even destruction. Men join sports teams, but may learn only to compete. They have sex with as many partners as possible, but remain lonely. They buy a gas guzzler and drive too fast without their seat belt. They over-consume tobacco, booze, and other drugs which poison their bodies. They purchase only products that prove they are "real" men. They physically fight each other. They work at their jobs until they drop over dead from heart failure. They buy a gun and shoot something or someone—or sometimes, themselves.

Wise societies provide much clearer, safer rites of passage into manhood. What men in America need are more gentle experiences of manhood: fishing, taking a walk with your father, and sitting in a barbershop listening to other men who are relaxed and happy being themselves. America is lacking in ritual and places for male bonding. Eric Fridman (1991), in an article titled "Haircut (Barbering in America is Becoming a Forgotten Art)," wrote:

There are, to be sure, not many of the old masculine ways left. The ready availability of food and the refinement of the science of food preservation have transformed hunting, which used to offer men frequent opportunities for fraternal camaraderie, from a stark necessity of life into a quaint archaism. Attendance at and participation in public sporting events, which once gave men the chance to enjoy the company of other men and to join together in support of common pleasures have in large part given way to solitary viewing in front of the television set.

Fridman goes on to recall the masculine world of the barbershop:

What I recall most about my early visits to Pat and Mike's [barbershop], however, are not so much the owners themselves as the reek of stale cigar smoke, the slap of straight razors against leather sharpening strops, and the

glint of chrome ashtrays placed next to each waiting chair. I remember also the magazines in the shop: *Field and Stream, Outdoor Life, Argosy* and the occasional *Police Gazette*, all of which offered intimate, sometimes lurid glimpses into the mysterious, exotic world of older men. Now, thirty years later, I've come to realize that my visits to Pat and Mike's provided me with my earliest clues about how grown-up men ought to look, speak, and act—how they ought to spend their leisure time, how they ought to regard women, what kinds of jokes they ought to tell. As an impressionable boy of five or six, I revered the men who gathered at this barbershop on Saturday morning, and mimicked their easy laughter and self-confident gestures. Once in a while I still meet such men today, usually in the course of my business dealings, and whenever I do, I regard them with the same peculiar mixture of admiration and awe I felt as a child.

The repetition of the barbering ritual every two or three weeks not only allows us to renew contact with our community, it also provides us with an opportunity to gain some measure of how our lives have changed or remained the same over the years.

As you read the remainder of this book, I invite you to think of the barbershop in a way that may be novel to you. Think of it as a place of community, kinship, affinity, and affirmation. When I asked one barber what time he closed on Saturdays, he responded: "Well, it depends on how our favorite team is doing. If we are winning, then I can close up early and watch the game at home. If they are losing that day, I stay open later because I know guys will be depressed and will want to come in for a trim or a cup of coffee."

One barber's philosophy on the attraction of traditional barbershops was summed up in one word. He stated, "I bet you would like to know why people still come to old-fashioned barbershops. It's not just to get a haircut. You can get your ears lowered in any of a thousand places. They come for the bullshit. That's right, the bullshit. It's hard to come by good *honest* bullshit anymore.

"And something like that is worth going out of a guy's way to get."

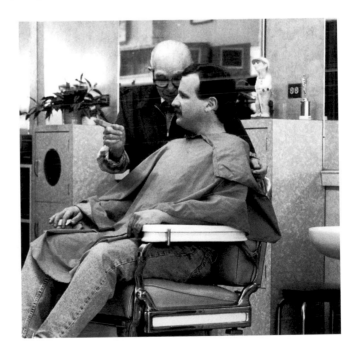

CHAPTER THREE

Through the Eyes of a Boy

"Barbers"
What they didn't expect
was how much they would love the place.
They didn't expect to love its
delicious sweet scent,
the deep trust of men,
the softness of that.
The talk was good, sure, and the work
easy compared to farming or mining,
the room always warm.
But whoever thought they'd wake up Sundays
and ache for the place just because they knew
it was heaven
and knew, shamefully,
miserable sinners that they were,
it was more than they deserved.
—Cynthia Rylant,
Something Permanent (1994)

Even as a child I knew there was something special—no, that is too mild a word—something sanctified about the local barbershop. But solemn it was not. I could clearly hear the men's voices and laughter as my mother and I approached the door. But as we entered it suddenly became silent. Clearly we had intruded. My mother had violated an unspoken rule. She had entered a man's place. The men stopped chatting and became engrossed in their newspapers or magazines, until she left. Meanwhile, my nose eagerly took in the smell of tobacco, aftershave, and the various mysterious potions for the grooming of hair. The scent of masculinity.

Some children hate having their hair cut. I remember quite the opposite. I loved getting my hair cut. For days afterwards I would rub the back of my neck to feel the texture of the growing fuzz where the barber's razor had sheared the hair. Someday I would have this sensation on my cheek and chin. I would be a man and shave. When I kissed my dad or one of my grandfathers goodnight, I was aware of

the texture of their cheeks, coarse from a day's growth of beard.

As I sat in the barbershop watching the barber working on a customer, I listened intently to the small talk he made. The topics were always the same. Sports were always popular, particularly baseball and football, but hockey too. Once in a while boxing. These were men who took their teams seriously. Men who had not physically taken part in a sporting event since high school—more years ago than I had been alive—talked about *their* teams. They took both defeat and victory personally. "How could they do that to us?" they asked one another after a particularly humiliating loss. With every victory, they talked with enthusiasm as if they each were the hero of the game.

It was always boisterous, unless it was World Series time. Then there was only the sound of the scissors, the AM radio, the hum of the lights, and the fan blowing as it gently moved from side to side in a feeble attempt to cool the stuffy room. Only when a commercial break came did anyone speak. Watching the men in the shop reminded me of scenes in old newsreels of World War II. Everyone was glued to the announcer's voice, hovering around the radio as if the crackly voice was giving the news of Pearl Harbor, or the invasion of Europe, or dropping "the big one." The World Series broadcasts seemed that important. They were certainly not treated as background noise. Each game was to be studied, contrasted with games of other years. Of course, few players of today could compare favorably with players in the "good old days—when men played for the love of the game,

not to become millionaires."

After team sports, the next most important topic was hunting. "Get your deer this year?" Not "Get *a* deer this year?" It was always "Get *your* deer this year?" As if there was a deer with your name out there just waiting for you to find it and shoot it. Then you tied its body to the trunk or roof of your big American automobile, and drove it home for all to see. "Let's cut through town on our way home. Just to see what's happenin'." Actually, just to make sure that everybody saw that you got your deer. To insure that everybody witnessed your success, you stopped at the cafe for a big, slow breakfast.

In you would march, loudly greeting anyone you knew. You swaggered through the cafe in hunting clothes—clothes worn for days as you had sat, or walked the fields and woods, waiting for your deer to show itself. Unshaven, smelling of stale beer, whiskey, and sweat, you proudly took your place at the largest table by the window. There, you could look out on your prize, draped over your car, and watch passersby admire it. Finally, you would go home, knowing that the details of the hunt could be reprised, blow by blow, for the guys at the barbershop.

When men at the barbershop spoke of hunting, particularly deer hunting, as if they were talking about a holy ritual. And of course, it was. For what occasions were we youngsters excused from school for two entire weeks? For Christmas—the birth of the son of the Christian God—and for the time of the deer "harvest."

The story and the haircut complete, one more time, the

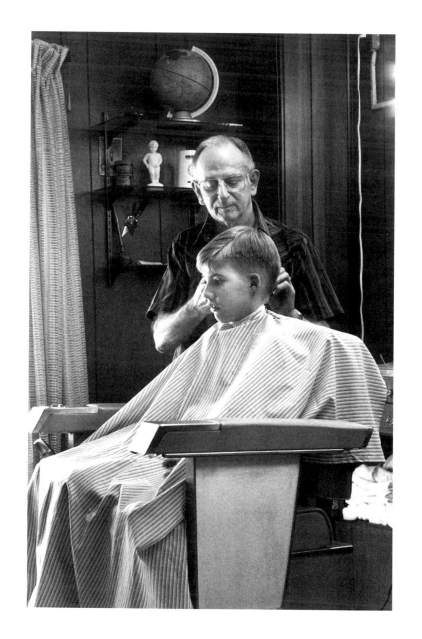

barber finished with his customer, rotating him around to view the results in the mirrors from all angles. Then the barber swept the hair off with the tiny broom, took the tissue paper from around his neck, and flung the white hair-cloth off, giving it a loud snap so the hair flew down onto the floor. Finally, he stepped over to the huge metal cash register to ring up the charge.

As the adult customer replaced his wallet in the back pocket of his work pants, I wondered, as the only child in the place, "Will this be the time?" The men sat in the wooden chairs that lined the walls in straight lines. The steam radiators clanked. A moment of silence hung in the air as the echoes of salutations just given the departing customer died out. The barber spoke, "Next." The moment of truth. Would this be the time?

Then the next man in line said those damned words, "Go ahead and take the boy. I can wait." Oh, I longed for the day I would have to wait my turn. To be just another of the men.

Once again my mother entered, back from the beauty salon. The bell rang and the plate-glass window shook as she shut the door behind her. Again the men became quiet and began paging through the mounds of magazines hot from sitting for hours on the radiators. The barber finished with me, removed the padded board on which I had been perched to make me tall enough for him to reach, took the money from my mother, and thanked her. The charge was another reminder that I was yet a boy. She paid him the "children's rate."

There were no good-natured insults as I left, as there had been for other customers leaving, only the sound of the barber's one-word invitation: "Next." Once the door closed behind my mother and me, the voices and the laughter began again.

One day it finally happened. I had grown old enough that my mother had just dropped me off on her way to an appointment at the beauty parlor. (Only women made appointments. Men took turns.) I made sure she dropped me off a block away from the shop, so that nobody would see that my mom had driven me. She had given me the money so I could pay the barber myself. As I entered, the men kept right on talking and laughing, but nodded at me as I passed and took my place at the end of the line of chairs. As had happened so many times before, the barber bid farewell to his customer, swept off the seat of the chair, and requested, "Next." I sadly rose to take my rightful place in the barber chair since I was the only boy in the room—when it finally happened. A man said, "Hey! Wait your turn, buddy. I'm next." I gladly sat down trying to hide my smile. I had made it. I was a man.

I went back to paging through *Field & Steam* and *Sports Illustrated*. The articles seem somehow to be less foreign than they had been only a few moments ago. The photographs were now of *other men*, like me.

Others have agreed that the barbershop is a place where the rituals of manhood are to be found. Peter Dimock, my colleague and friend, has told me how he anxiously awaited the day that the barber would lather the back of Peter's neck and shave it with a straight razor. To him, and the other boys

in his town, that was a sign of adulthood. The hair on the backs of boys' necks were merely trimmed with the clippers. Only men had their necks shaved. Peter recalled how surprised he was the first time the barber wordlessly applied the foam to his neck, and the sound and feel of the blade as it moved across his skin. He also recalled the smile he wore as he proudly strode out of the barbershop and sauntered down the street, somehow taller and stronger than he had been when he entered the shop.

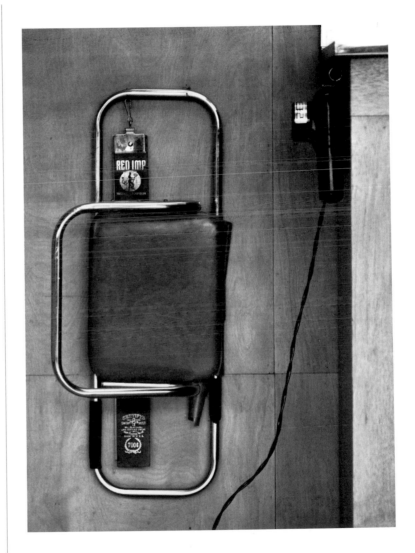

CHAPTER FOUR

Of Tonics and Smells

One time a fellow says to me "Don't put that stuff in my hair.
When I go home my wife will think I've been in a whorehouse."
The guy in the next chair says,
"Put it on my hair,
my wife doesn't know what it smells like in a whorehouse."
—*Vern Swanson,*
From the Barber's Chair

Remember being a young student in elementary school, pressing the test paper close to your nose—so you could inhale the scent given off by the freshly-printed purple ditto paper? How quickly can you bring to mind the childhood smell of crayons, or white paste? Or, if you are from a more recent generation, what about the pungent whiff of drawing with Magic Markers? Think of your favorite holiday; does the enticing aroma of Mom's or Grandma's cooking fill your nose?

Advertisers know the power of scents to trigger emotions. How many ads show images that suggest both sex and fragrances? Or use advertising copy that speaks of the scent of masculinity—smelling like a man? An old ad jingle for pipe tobacco went "Smells grand, packs right, smokes sweet, can't bite." First among the singers' promises was the grand aroma.

Although smells are a powerful trigger for memories, one rarely hears references to the sense of smell in polite conversation—unless of course the topic is barbershops. Then,

odoriferous recollections come pouring out. Barbershops are fragrant with witch hazel, Old Spice, Aqua-Velva, and pipe tobacco. These are smells comforting to men—or anyone who has loved a man, a father, a brother, a grandfather. To a boy wanting to become a man, they are magical fragrances indeed.

One test of adolescence is to understand the difference between aftershave and cologne. For those who have not broken the code, I will let you in on the secret. Aftershave is a scented, but astringent liquid applied to the skin following shaving (hence the name). The aftershave causes the pores to contract (after they have been opened by hot towels or hot water applied before shaving to soften the beard). Cologne is a mixture of aromatic oils applied to the skin for the purpose of smelling good. (I was always taught that gentlemen wear "cologne," while ladies wear "perfume.")

Prior to the development of brand-name commercial aftershaves, barbers applied witch hazel to the customers' cheeks following shaving. Witch hazel is distilled from the witch-hazel bush. The recipe also included water and grain alcohol. During the years of Prohibition, brewers commonly made a type of non-alcoholic "near-beer" by brewing regular beer and then removing the alcohol. This excess alcohol was then sold to manufacturers of inferior grades of witch hazel and other tonics. The beer-based alcohol was used in tonic formulas instead of higher-grade grain alcohol to cut costs. However, although other ingredients were added to cover up the beer smell, once applied to the skin the masking scents soon evaporated, and the customer was left smelling like beer (*Krank's Review*, June 1925). In those days, such a scent could have gotten a man in as much trouble as smelling of marijuana would today.

I always knew when my father was going out with my mother. I would hear the distinctive sound of him, in the bathroom, rubbing aftershave on his palms and slapping it on his cheeks. It was the same sound he made every morning after he shaved, but in the evening he skipped the shaving part. "I'll just dab on some aftershave, and make everyone think I shaved again for the party," he would announce for the millionth time—as if my brother and I had never witnessed this Friday night ritual.

This is the main drawback I have discovered to my wearing a beard. If I shaved each morning, I would be reminded daily of my father as I slapped the stinging liquid to my cheeks freshly scraped by a razor.

CHAPTER FIVE

Barber Chairs

It is like a barber's chair
that fits all buttocks.
—*William Shakespeare,*
All's Well That Ends Well

I had recently moved into a new house and, at a friend's party, was passing around some snapshots. When the photographs of our den—complete with a barber chair— were shown, I noticed some interesting reactions. Universally the females exclaimed to my wife, "You let him *keep* that thing *in the house*?" All they saw was a large, very heavy chair. But the men had the strongest reaction. They all said, "*Where did you get it? I've always wanted a barber chair!*" One elderly man went so far to say, "If I had a barber chair, I would build a room just to put it in. I would go and sit in it anytime I wanted to relax and think. Some of the most enjoyable times in my life have been sitting in a barber chair—just talking and listening. I can't think of a better place to be!"

After witnessing the reactions (at least the male ones), I could see why antique barber chairs are so expensive. When first searching for the chair I now own, I began by wandering through antique stores. The chairs I found were fetching over $1,000 (and this was ten years ago). This price was too

rich for my taste, so I began to visit small-town barbershops, asking if they had a chair for sale. This is how this book really got started—as a search for a barber chair for my den.

After a couple of years without results, I stopped in a shop where a barber had not one, but two chairs of the style I wanted. I asked if he would be willing to part with one. He said he could never sell either chair, as he had promised that when he retired they would be sold with the shop to a man who planned to open a hair salon and wanted them as decorations. As I disappointedly began to leave, he added that he also owned an identical chair which was at home. He could be convinced to sell it "if the price was right."

When I asked what that price might be, he reminded me that it was in mint condition. He had to get top dollar for it since it had been in his family for years. In my mind, the price tag was growing ever larger by the second. Until he said, "Yup, I'd have to get fifty dollars. And don't try to talk me down either." I handed him $50, and drove to a nearby town (50 miles away) to rent a trailer.

When I arrived home with my prize, I had no trouble finding men in the neighborhood to help me carry it downstairs to the den. If you want a great gimmick to gather a crowd of men rapidly—even better than raising the hood of your car and sticking your head under it—try pulling up to your house with an antique barber chair in a trailer.

Traditional barber chairs were built to last. I was in numerous shops where the chairs still in use were 80 to 100 years old. Barber chairs have to be tough. They have to be able to hold a man of any size and still be very comfortable. They are constantly in use, if not by a customer then often by the barber himself. Next time you walk past a barbershop, glance in the window. If the barber is not working on a customer, you can bet he will probably be sitting in his chair—eating, napping, or reading.

Another reason traditional barber chairs had to be strong and well balanced was because they reclined to allow the barber to shave a customer. Next time you are in a barbershop, note the massive base of the chair. Its great weight and low center of gravity allow the chair to comfortably support even the largest man. Modern chairs, like those used in hair salons, are not built as ruggedly and do not have the huge base; they can not be elevated as high as barber chairs. Therefore stylists may have to bend over to reach their clients, while barbers can simply pump the hydraulic handle and raise the customer to a comfortable working height.

A barber once gave me several points of advice concerning barber chairs:

Always buy two chairs right away, even when opening a one-man shop. That way if you want to expand, you won't have chairs that are unmatched in style or color.

In addition, it is a good idea to have one chair for use in the summer. That way you and the customer can be farther from the window and the hot sunlight, and closer to the air conditioner. The other chair is put closer to the radiator and used in the winter to stay warm.

Also, having one more chair than the number of barbers currently employed gives a positive message to the customers. It suggests that the owner expects to expand his business. Everyone wants to be associated with a business that is perceived as growing.

Boys' hair used to be cut in special chairs. Some children's chairs were merely smaller versions of adult chairs, but some were very different. An 1929 ad in *Krank's Review* sang the praises of one such chair: the Koch's Hydraulic Child's Chair (#43). It looked like a small car, manufactured with:

> all modern accessories of a real automobile: rubber tires on steel wheels, windshield with mirror, horn on the steering-wheel column, head-lights, spot light, self-starter which can be wound up, bumper in front, brake and trunk with hinged lid, upholstered leather seat, all combine to make the outfit decidedly realistic.

All this was painted in "bright colors." Of course, the car was mounted on an adjustable base so the child's head could be raised to the appropriate height for the barber.

When a barber faces cutting a very young boy's hair, especially for the first time—and without the advantage of a wonderful distraction like Koch's Hydraulic Child's Chair #43—there are three schools of thought:

1. Don't do it at all. Let somebody else cut his hair until he is old enough to sit still and not cry.
2. Strap him in securely—a large man's belt will generally do the trick.
3. Use bribery. A sucker works best—as long as you make sure he keeps it out of his hair.

56

CHAPTER SIX

Barber Poles

"As modern as a jet plane.
Draws customers like honey draws bees."
—*from the catalog of the William Marvy Co.*

Long before the days of corporate logos, various trades had symbols associated with their services. These were essential as a good percentage of citizens were illiterate and could not read signs with words. The history of the barber pole dates back to the days when a barber was responsible for more than cutting hair. Shaves, tooth extraction, and blood-letting were also available. In the western half of America, barbers were still responsible for extracting teeth well into the 1800s. And as late as 1913, a barber in St. Louis was still offering leeching as a service (Krumholz, 1989).

The shape of the bottom of the classic barber pole is similar to the shape of the container used for holding blood-letting leeches. The pole itself is said to be derived from the wooden pole a patron clenched while undergoing a painful procedure. The red and white stripes are said to represent the bloody bandages, hung out to dry, which were twisted around the stake to which they were tied. Some claim the blue stripe denotes the blood in the veins; others say it merely was added to the red and white stripes by Americans

to be more patriotic. In England, Lord Thurlow, in a speech to the House of Peers in 1797, spoke in support of a bill to allow both barbers and surgeons to use poles as trademarks. However, the barbers were to use a pole that was blue-and-white striped, while the surgeons were to use red and white stripes (Andrews, 1904).

Prior to the 1930s, barber poles were large and free-standing on the sidewalk. But by the 1940s, sidewalk space was considered too valuable, and local ordinances prevented new poles from being installed. At that time the now-familiar, smaller glass-encased poles became popular. Even this style of barber pole is now disappearing, due to vandals breaking the glass. Replacement and repair can be costly. A typical glass cylinder costs $50 to $130 to replace (it takes a lot of haircuts to pay that bill). Depending on size and features, a completely new pole costs between $350 and $800. Many barbers who still display glass barber poles now place them inside their windows to protect them from damage or theft.

It was not until the early part of the century that barber poles came to have the now-classic rotating cylinder. Prior to 1925, a hand-wound clock-like mechanism turned the striped cylinder. A single winding kept the pole rotating for up to twelve hours. By the 1930s, newly manufactured poles were turned by electric motors. A sharp-eyed observer can often spot a building which used to contain a barbershop by noting the remnants of the hardware once used to fasten and power the barber pole.

Although barber poles were used as early as the 14th cen-tury, it was not until the 1900s that they were mass-produced. Prior to that time each pole was made by hand, usually of wood, and then painted. At one time there were four national and two regional barber-pole factories in America alone. Now there are only three places in the entire world that manufacture poles. They are found in Japan, Italy, and America. The one plant that supplies all of North America is the William Marvy Company of St. Paul, Minnesota.

William Marvy got his start by doing odd jobs at a barber-supply company in St. Paul where his sister was the bookkeeper. He ran the mimeograph machine, addressed fliers, stirred vats of hair tonic, and delivered orders to barbers by riding the street cars. When he was old enough to drive he got promoted to city driver, replacing a man with an excessive affection for consuming alcohol during working hours. In 1936, after rising to the position of salesman on a five-day traveling route, William was laid off when the company decided to sell exclusively by mail. He decided to work for himself and took to the back roads of rural Minnesota selling barber supplies, including poles, which he bought directly from manufacturers.

In 1950, on New Year's Day, he completed his own plans to manufacture a pole that was "six-ways-better" than the poles he had been selling. One improvement included replacing the paper cylinder with an acetate that resisted fading from the sunlight. His models also included stainless-steel domes and bowls, easier to maintain than the older porcelain-covered cast iron. A reporter from the *Wall Street Journal* reviewed his pole in 1950 and stated it was "the first

real improvement in the barber pole in a quarter of a century" (Legler, 1985). The ad for the Marvy 99 claimed that when it came to attracting customers, the pole had "more pulling power than the Pied Piper." The most popular model, the Marvy 55, was claimed to "stop the eye and start the sale."

At one time Mr. Marvy had a staff of fourteen people working to produce 5,000 poles a year. Marvy made his 50,000th pole in 1968. To mark the occasion, his employees built a special gold-and-white striped pole and threw a party. Marvy produced over 74,000 poles since opening his own factory in 1950. For this feat he was elected to the Barber Hall of Fame—quite an honor for someone who had never given anyone a haircut.

Well into his 80s, the man everyone called "Mr. Marvy" still came into the plant everyday, just to make sure everything was running smoothly. Asked just one question about poles, he would gladly launch into a well-practiced monologue on the history of the barber trade that he had delivered before to reporters from *National Geographic* to *Ripley's Believe It or Not!*

Bill Marvy passed away in 1993. His duties have been taken over by his son, Bob. Today there are twelve models of poles available. There are poles with the words "hair stylist" printed on one of the stripes. Another model for dog groomers has leaping pink poodles. The company, now diversified, has a staff of eighteen people and produces 500 poles per year, a level fairly constant for the last ten years. Each employee is skilled at several different jobs. A person may be called on to do shipping, receiving, pole repair, cylinder cutting, product packing, answering the phone, or waiting on walk-in customers. Apparently it is an enjoyable place to work. The most senior employee has been there 41 years.

Unless destroyed by fire or stolen, a barber pole is a once-in-a-lifetime purchase. The repair department at the William Marvy Company commonly gets poles built around the turn of the century. These venerable poles are fixed and returned ready to provide additional decades of assistance to the barber.

With the decline in barbershops, today there are actually more barber poles than barbers. Many are used by non-barbers for decoration in bars or home dens. For example, Skitch Henderson, the band leader, is known to have an impressive collection of barber poles in his home. Since poles have become a collector's item, the Marvy Company now takes out ads in antique magazines as well as barber journals.

Each year Marvy's repair department get busier due to the increasing number of collectors sending in poles to be refurbished. Bob told me that he can always tell if a damaged pole was sent in by a collector or a practicing barber. The collector is willing to pay any price; the barber always wants an estimate to be sure the repair would cost less than a new pole.

My Boyhood Education Continues

No beauty she doth miss,
when all her robes are on;
But beauty's self she is,
when all her robes are gone.
—*English madrigal*

Like a lot of boys, when I was young I was fascinated, but confused, about the differences between men and women. I already had most of the technical information about where babies came from. In fact I got sent to the principal's office for knowing this. Actually, not for merely knowing, but for saying what I knew out loud.

I had been invited to play house by one of my classmates. She said she would be the mommy and I could be the daddy. I concurred. The trouble began when she decided that we should have a baby. I don't recall how she thought babies came about, but I do remember telling her the version I had been told by my parents (the one I still believe to this day). She was horrified that I would suggest that her parents had taken part in the act I had described in such graphic, yet accurate fashion, and ran to the teacher to inform her of my evilness.

I was not upset up to this point. My parents had taught me that teachers were people to be trusted. I was sure that my teacher also knew the basic facts about human repro-

duction, and would assure my fellow student that I was completely correct.

To my surprise, I was sent to see the principal. Even at this point, I was calm. I knew that the principal had to be a man of reason and science to have risen to such a position of authority. Besides, other than the maintenance man, he was the only adult male in the whole school, so he would understand and naturally side with me.

You can imagine my dismay when he began to scold me for having a dirty mind and frightening my classmate. He ordered me never to speak of such things again or I would not be welcome at the school. I was aghast. How could this be? How could the truth be frightening or dangerous? How dare he threaten my school career—which had only begun and still had a long way to go? Had I not merely spoken the facts?

However, I can also recall noting at an early age that the differences between men and women went further than who contributed what to the fertilization process. There were role differences. For example, cooking was women's work—if it was done within the home. However, the preparation of food *outdoors* became men's work. Women required specialized tools for handling food, particular types of pots, and such. Men cooked over fire. Give a man an open flame, a fork, and a piece of animal flesh and he will make a meal out of it.

I also noticed that only women carried purses. In fact, the older they got, the bigger grew the purses they lugged about. My grandmother's purse could have held a medium-size dog (if she had liked dogs). In it, among countless items, she carried several folded rain-bonnets. It was clear to me that men didn't need rain-bonnets; they could get their hair wet.

In fact, men did not need purses because they used their pockets to carry things. Men's pockets had change in them that made noise when they walked—or even when they stood still, because they put their hands in their pockets and clinked coins together while they talked. Obviously, the coins were very significant.

And men had wallets. Not those big brightly-colored wallets with coin purses like women. Men had folding black or brown leather wallets that they kept for years, even a lifetime. Despite getting a new wallet for Father's Day, they would keep using the old ones. They filled their old, worn wallets with money, important papers, and maybe a picture of the wife and kids—or a particularly big fish caught on a trip "up North." But they definitely did not have those fold-out plastic photo-holders like women's wallets had.

It will be no surprise to learn that from a very young age, I made a practice of having change in my pocket. Not to spend, mind you, but to clank to announce my manhood to everyone within earshot. Also, a wallet appeared in my hip pocket long before I had a dollar bill to fold in it. But the personal information on the I.D. card that came with it was filled in completely. Typed, in fact, by my mother, who apparently understood the need of her boy to become a man as fast as possible.

But though my parents made sure that I had the facts about human reproduction, and despite my own early obser-

vations of gender-based behavior, there was still something missing in my understanding of differences between men and women. I understood the role of different parts in reproduction, yet I wasn't sure exactly what they looked like.

As I got older, I found myself becoming increasingly more curious about human anatomy—especially in the presence of a certain female relative when she was wearing a particularly tight pink sweater. The library had all the "good books" (the ones with photographs) in a special locked case that could only be opened by the librarian. She had the nasty habit of asking very loudly (whatever happened to whispering in the library?), "Young man, does your *mother* know you want to look at those kind of books?"

I tried saying, "Yes, she encourages me to learn all I can about whatever subject I am interested in." However, she did not fall for it, and said she would believe me when she saw a note signed by my parents. I can just see the note now: "Dear Sir or Madam, please allow my son to view as many books containing detailed photographs of naked women as you have available in your collection."

My peer group was of little help in my quest for knowledge. I never ran into anyone who wanted to "play doctor." My elementary school teachers were not helpful. They always made sure that when we lay down on the gym floor to do exercises that the boys faced away from the girls, so we could not look up their skirts for some hint of what all the fuss was about.

It was the barbershop, not the school system, that was to be the source of my education on this matter. The teaching came in the form of a magazine. The barbershop always had magazines scattered about. I could look through a magazine at my leisure and never worry about not finishing an article. The issues stacked up for years. If I didn't finish an article, it would be there the next haircut—and the haircut after that, and the one after that. The magazines fell apart before they were thrown out.

One day, as was I excavating some of the more ancient magazines from the bottom of the stack, the ones hot from lying on the radiator, I stumbled on a treasure: a "girlie" magazine. I knew I would have to forsake the centerfold, but there were riches enough between those two covers. Carefully, I nonchalantly slid my find into another magazine to disguise it. I stared transfixed at the photographs of a completely—well almost—naked female person. So that what they look like. The mystery was solved.

I figured I had been clever enough to have fooled everyone in the shop, until I looked up—and they were looking at me, smiling. I had forgotten that the wall behind me was covered with mirrors, and the reflection of the photos was clear to everyone in the place. The barber paused long enough to give me a wink, and went back to the snip, snip, snip of the scissors.

I was embarrassed at being caught, but this soon faded as I realized that no one was going to stop me. Now this was the final proof that I was a man. For a moment, I thought about taking the magazine with me when I left, but thought wiser of it and left with my haircut and my memories.

68

CHAPTER EIGHT
Hair and Hairstyles

You can't imagine how bad some people's hair looks.
There is no way of looking bad that hair hasn't tried.
—*Roy Blount (1986)*

Confrontational and flyaway, or fashionable and sculpted,
hair style speaks.
It's capable of wit, lust, aggression, and irony.
Organic yet malleable into the most unnatural states.
—*G. Hirshev (1987)*

Vir pilosus, seu fortis, seu libidinosus.
A Roman saying—
"The hairy man is either strong or lustful."
—*Wendy Cooper (1971)*

Sometimes, you like to let the hair do the talking.
—*James Brown (in Blount, 1986)*

I could not write about barbers and barbering without also writing about hair. Where would barbers be without hair? Blood-letting and putting leeches on people, no doubt. For that matter, where would any of us be without hair? Humorist Roy Blount (1986) suggested that fussing with hair might lie at the very root of civilization. His theory holds that back at some point in evolution, early pre-humans had to keep tossing their heads back to keep their hair out of their eyes. The longer the hair, the more they used their front legs to kick at the hair, and this caused them to put more weight on their hind legs. Eventually they learned to stand upright. The first barber probably set up shop soon after, using a sharp rock to hack off the offending portions of these locks.

The importance of hair continues to this day. Americans spent 2.5 billion dollars on services and products for their hair in one year (*New York Times*, July 1, 1985).

What is the big deal about hair anyway? We have incorporated references to hair in our very language, especially to

refer to fine measurements: hair breadth, hair splitting, hair trigger. When someone suffers a penance, we say he is wearing a hair shirt. Anyone who has gotten hair down his back during a haircut can tell you the idea of an entire shirt made of hair is a frightening image. Speaking of frightening, hair-raising is a synonym for horrifying.

Hair is found only on mammals. Some species have hair grouped in a characteristic pattern. Humans (along with cows and horses) have no follicle groups; our hair is evenly distributed throughout the skin (Ryder, 1973). Although *Homo sapiens* has been called the "naked ape" by zoologist Desmond Morris (1967), we still are fairly hairy, some of us more than others. We do have fewer hairs per square centimeter than gibbons and gorillas, but in fact have three times more than the chimpanzee (Firth, 1973). The reason that those primates look hairier is because our hair is finer and shorter than theirs (W. Cooper, 1971). So next time you watch *Bedtime for Bonzo*, just remember that Ronald Reagan, hair-wise, is more dense than his anthropoid co-star.

The characteristics of hair vary among races. Mongolians, including American Indians, Chinese, Eskimos and Japanese, have coarser, straighter scalp hair, with relatively little facial or body hair. Negroes tend to be more hairy, but the hair on their heads is not usually straight. Caucasoids are the hairiest people of all. They also have hair that can be straight, wavy, or curly. The type of hair a race has is related to what part of the world they originally inhabited. Those from climates with intense sunlight have more pigment in their skin and darker hair to reduce damage caused by ultra-violet radiation. The inhabitants of more temperate areas of the globe are more likely to have lighter skin and hair color (W. Cooper, 1971).

Hair is very functional. It provides mechanical protection from wear and tear. It is usually found on areas of the body where the skin is thinner. Eyelashes and hair in the nostrils and ears protect us from the intrusion of objects. Hair also provides thermal insulation, so it makes sense that most of us have hair on our heads where we lose twenty percent of our body heat.

Public hair and axillary hair (under the arms) is functional as well. It protects against friction where body parts are likely to rub together. But there must be more to it than that, because, unlike on our scalp, hair in these areas does not appear until we reach puberty. Why does the body wait until sexual maturity to grow hair in certain areas? It may have more to do with the fact that scent glands are found at these locations. The hair provides a surface to hold the glands' secretions, so they can oxidize gradually into the surrounding air and act as a sexual stimulant. Or at least they did in the past. Today, we attempt to eliminate or cover up these scents.

For humans, hair on the top of the head has become more than functional way of covering the skin. Much more!

Once the human race discovered that hair was good-tempered, pliable, and regenerative, and could be cut, shaved, shaped, dyed, braided, crimped, curled, waved, puffed, padded, and frizzled, it proceeded to use hair in a

vast variety of permutations of length, style, and color, in the long, continuous search for novelty, beauty, and status sometimes called fashion. [W. Cooper, 1971]

It is striking to note how out of this sluggish, physiologically almost functionless appurtenance of his body, man has imaginatively created a feature of such social differentiating and symbolic power. It is detachable, renewable, manipulable in many contexts, so to some degree can be treated as an independent object. And it is associative, tending to call up important social ideas, especially concerning sex. [Firth, 1973]

Hair is frequently thought of as a very sexual part of the body, as haircare ads remind us. Therefore, it makes sense that those who lead a celibate lifestyle, such as monks, shave their hair. Nuns traditionally covered their hair with a habit (Synott, 1987). We may be evolutionarily wired to find healthy hair sexy. When a person is weakened by digestive or circulatory problems, this can affect the appearance of scalp hair. Hairs begin to split, and there is a loss of flexibility, color, and glossiness, sometimes leading to major hair-loss (De Zemler, 1939). Perhaps ancient *Homo sapiens* who did not pay attention to the condition of their potential mates' hair ended up with sickly partners unable to reproduce or survive to care for their young. In contrast, those distant ancestors who were hair conscious found healthier mates, were more fruitful, and multiplied.

It is interesting to note that hair grows at a faster rate when a person is between the age of 17 and 24, when most people are looking for mates (De Zemler, 1939). If hair were merely designed to keep your head warm, you would expect it to grow faster in the winter and slower in the summer. But the opposite is true. Cold weather slows the growth of hair (De Zemler, 1939). So there must be more to hair than providing warmth.

Certainly hair and sex seem to go together in many people's minds. Perhaps its ability to regenerate itself makes it a handy symbol of renewal, fertility, and virility (W. Cooper, 1971). As sociologist Anthony Synnott (1987) wrote:

Hair is perhaps our most powerful symbol of individual and group identity—powerful first because it is physical and therefore extremely personal, and second because, although personal, it is also public rather than private. Furthermore, hair symbolism is usually voluntary rather than imposed or "given." Finally, hair is malleable, in various ways, and therefore singularly apt to symbolize both differentiation between, and changes in, individual and group identities.

Anthropologist E.A. Leach (1958) believes that long hair is a sign of unrestrained sexuality. Therefore short hair, a partially shaved head, or tightly bound hair is symbolic of restricted sexuality, and a closely shaven head is a sign of celibacy. Psychiatrist Charles Berg (1951), trained from a psychoanalytic perspective, suggested that the human head

symbolically equals the phallus (the penis or clitoris, but particularly the penis) and the hair is representative of semen. It then follows that haircutting is a form of castration (in Hallpike, 1969). Now there is a viewpoint I bet they do not teach in barber school. If Dr. Berg is right then it is no wonder a boy's first haircut tends to be traumatic.

Sociologist C.R. Hallpike (1969) took this information and concluded that a man having his hair cut short is a sign of social control, while wearing his hair long is a sign of being outside of society. This explains why those under a great deal of social control, such as soldiers, monks, and convicts, have short hair. At the other extreme are the long hairs: intellectuals, artists, and juvenile rebels, all on the fringe of society's control.

Hair has been viewed as a sign of physical strength. The Old Testament story of Samson (*Judges 13–16*) tells the familiar story of the man who was fantastically strong—until he allowed his locks to be shorn which caused him to become weak. In his weakened state, he was defeated by his enemies and thrown into a dungeon. (You think you have had bad haircut experiences.) There he rotted until his hair grew back, at which time he is reported to have thrown quite a fit.

The North American Sioux also believed hair was the center of strength, so by scalping their enemies they insured that the fallen warriors could not harm the victor after death. The claimed scalp served as a token of manhood. For their part, White bounty hunters were required to produce a scalp as proof of a killing before being paid (W. Cooper, 1971).

Hair has also been seen as a wellspring of mental ability. The Greek philosopher, Pythagoras, taught that the hair was the source of the brain's inspiration. Therefore, one's thinking ability decreased when the hair was cut. The belief that there is a connection between hair and intelligence persists to this day. According to John Molloy, author of the 1988 book, *Dress for Success*, businessmen think that men who part their hair on the side of their head are brighter, harder working, and make better employees than those who part their hair down the middle.

Hair is a very personal thing. Parents frequently keep hairs from their baby's first haircut. Lovers exchange locks of hair. Fans of popular culture figures such as film actors or musicians often try to obtain locks of hair as a souvenir. This has been going on for a long time. The Hungarian classical composer Franz Liszt (1811–1886) had a barber who made a small fortune selling locks of the composer's hair to those who idolized him (De Zemler, 1939). Souvenir hair-buying continues in this century as well. A lock of hair that had belonged to British naval hero Lord Horatio Nelson (1758–1805) was sold in Great Britain in 1988 for £5,575, or roughly $10,000 (McFarlan, 1992).

Seeking to understand the symbolism of hairstyles, Pat MacDonald of the band *Timbuk 3* posed a series of musical questions:

> Hairstyles and attitudes, are they connected?
> Are styles we embrace a matter of taste, or values rejected?

Hairstyles and attitudes, how do they relate?

How well do we use our freedom to choose the illusions we create?

Blow dry, bouffant, basic training, cops in drag dressed up like whores,

Cowboys in pony tails, bankers in bangs, presidents in pompous pompadours,

Mommas in Mohawks, daddies in dreadlocks, heavy metal Goldilocks, trying to look tough,

The wet look, the dry look, the F.B.I. look.

But can you judge a crook by his cover-up?

[Mamdaddi Music Inc./IRS Music Inc.]

In simplest terms, hair is important to us because, second perhaps only to clothes, it is one of the easiest ways to change our appearance. Except by getting a new hairstyle, it is difficult to change your physical appearance. The most expensive haircut is a great deal less costly than the cheapest cosmetic surgery. And the recovery time from a bad haircut is nothing compared to getting over a bad face-lift. Admit it, getting a haircut is a mood-altering experience. Human beings are notorious for doing all kinds of things to change the way we feel. We will eat, drink, or smoke noxious substances just to feel differently. Getting a haircut is among the least dangerous and cheapest mood changes available. Hey, if you are about to relapse and blow your sobriety, but can not find an Alcoholics Anonymous meeting, get your hair cut. You will feel better, look better, and not end up in jail or wrapping your car around a telephone pole at the side of the road.

Don King, a professional boxing promoter known for his wild upswept hairstyle, had this to say about the vitality of hair:

I used to have my hair cut off and be glad about it. The barber would clip, clip, clip and snip, snip, snip. But even then, while my hair was dying on the vine, I felt its power. It got under my skin, up around my neck and behind my ears, making me uncomfortable and causing me terrible mental frustration. Oh, the horror! Even after the barber brushed my neck and shook talcum on it, the little hairs would still be crawling around my back, shouting, "Why did you do this to me, sir? Why did you kill me? Come back! I'm still alive! Get me!" Hair that's cut fights back. It rebels! And it always gets the last laugh, continuing to grow even when the rest of you is laid out on the slab. [Lidz, 1990]

With hair that rowdy, I can see why he makes his living encouraging large men to get into a ring and punch each other until one of them is unconscious. It makes me wonder what kind of work he would be involved with if he were bald.

Mr. L. Sherman Trusty (with a name like that, I tend to believe what he says) authored in 1960 a standard textbook of barbering, *The Art and Science of Barbering*. In it, he identified a number of factors throughout time that influenced hairstyles:

1. Historical characters who "either by popularity or mandate set the fashions of beards, shaving, haircutting, and mustaches." Trusty noted some of the leading fad setters of the last few years: "Moses, Alexander the Great, Hadrian, Charlemagne, and William, Archbishop of Roven." Charlemagne, by the way, was described elsewhere as being tall and strong with beautiful, well-combed flowing hair, often scented "if the moment called for it," with a reputation for "virility and sexual appetite"; he had four wives and at least five mistresses (W. Cooper, 1971).

Trusty's book was published in 1960, a few years before another quartet of fashion-setters could have been added to his list: John, Paul, George, and Ringo. My high-school principal, Harry Beulke, freaked out if anyone showed up with a Beatle haircut. Imagine his reaction if a Moses look-alike craze had swept the school.

2. Climatic conditions. As you might expect, colder climates favor longer hair than hairstyles in warmer climates. If true, then global warming has some serious hairstyle implications.

3. Race, nationality, and ethnic identity. Simply, different strokes (of the brush) for different folks.

4. Religion. Thou shalt wear thy hair thusly (or words to that effect).

5. Education. Trusty states that "The educated man is more likely to be interested in his appearance." How exactly does Albert Einstein fit this theory?

6. Customs. "Compliance with the customs is almost imperative if one is to live without friction."

7. The discovery of electricity and invention of electric implements.

A man can change the appearance of his hair in several ways. He can change the color with dyes and bleaches, or he can use artificial hair or wigs. But these methods are not without risk. Tertullian, a early Christian churchman of the 3rd century A.D., stated that "all personal disguise is adultery before God." If that were not bad enough, he also pointed out the dangers of using a wig: it may have been made with hair from a criminal, from someone with a dirty head, or from the scalp of someone already damned (W. Cooper, 1971). St. Clemens of Alexandria, circa 1600 A.D., warned that any man who was wearing a wig while kneeling at the alter was putting his soul at risk. He believed that a wig prevented God's blessing from reaching the head of the wearer (De Zemler, 1939).

The Great Plague of 1665 brought up the issue of wig safety once again. Wig makers were looking for a handy and cheap source of hair. Since the recently-dead victims of the illness had no use for their locks, the wig makers gladly recycled the hair in wig construction. Unfortunately for the wigmakers' customers, insects responsible for transmitting the plague were not nearly as dead as the people from whom the hair had been taken and happily infected the new owner of the wig (W. Cooper, 1971).

Hairstyles can also be powerful political statements. Famous communist revolutionaries such as Marx, Lenin,

Ho Chi Minh, and Fidel Castro all wore whiskers. In the 1960s, American men called Hippies grew their hair long as a protest against gender roles and the Viet Nam War. Following the Hippies came the Skinheads, who not only rejected the Establishment, but also rejected the Hippies as effeminate, lazy, and weak. As a sign of their opposition, Skinheads cut their hair very short. What hairstyle could the next group use as a symbol of protest? Along came Punks, with hair short and long at the same time—plus brightly colored in green, purple, and orange. To take the shock value further, they added spikes or shaved patterns in their scalp hair (Synott, 1987).

Writing about the politics of hair, Anthony Synnott (1987) noted that opposite ideologies usually wear opposite hairstyles. Hairstyles act like uniforms, so you can tell who is on your side and who is the bad guy. On the other hand (or head), two individuals may share the same hairstyle but for very different reasons. For example, a Skinhead and a Marine recruit look the same but the motives for the style are dissimilar.

Politically-influenced hairstyles are nothing new. In early 17th century France, full beards were customarily worn—until King Louis XIII was crowned at a very young age and was unable to grow a beard. As soon as he assumed the throne, it became politically correct to see the nearest barber and bid one's beard *adieux* (De Zemler, 1939).

In some cases, hairstyles are imposed on people. While leading the Jews out of Egypt, Moses decreed that haircuts and shaving were forbidden. "You should not round off your hair from side to side, and you shall not shave the edge of your beard" (*Leviticus 19:27*). Perhaps he wanted to protect his followers' heads from the rays of the sun, and hoped to save water, as they wandered in the desert for forty years. In more modern times, those who collaborated with the Nazi in France during World War II had their heads shaved by those angry with them. In Northern Ireland, the same treatment was given to Catholic women who dated British soldiers or Protestant men, to punish them and mark them as outcasts (Synott, 1987).

A man can change his appearance by changing the length of his hair. He can go for the short look—shaving his head and face—or go to the other extreme. *The Guinness Book of Records* (1992) reports that Mata Jagdamba, who currently lives in Ujjain, North India, has scalp hair that is 21 feet long. If you are thinking you might try to beat that record, you might note that human scalp hair grows at the rate of one-half to one inch per month (Blount, 1986).

Hans Steiniger of Austria grew his beard longer than his body. Unfortunately, he tripped over it while going down some stairs and tumbled to his death (W. Cooper, 1971). The longest beard on record belonged to Hans Langseth of Norway. His whiskers measured 17½ feet when he died in 1927. Since most men's beard hairs grow at a rate of six and one-half inches per year, it was calculated that he had not shaved for at least 32 years (De Zemler, 1939). After his death, Mr. Langseth's kin were so kind as to donate his beard in 1967 to the Smithsonian Institution in Washington, D.C. Birger Pellas, who is still alive in Malmö, Sweden, at the

time of this writing, is carrying around a ten foot mustache attached to his face. He has been growing it since 1973. What is it about these Scandinavian Vikings and their wild hair?

The very color of hair has cultural meaning for us. Fair hair is often seen as a cue of mild temper, calm judgment, and tender affections. Black hair is thought to be a sign of strong passions, vigor, and ambition (De Zemler, 1939). If this is true, does it explain the manner most people interact, considering the world is populated mainly by dark-haired people?

Certainly, people show strong attraction to others based on hair color. In the Old Testament's *Song of Solomon*, a woman praises her lover's hair, saying: "His head is as the most fine gold, his locks are bushy, and black as a raven." In a survey by *Glamour Magazine* (August 1983), 75% of American women stated that they preferred men with black or brown hair. Another 13% liked blondes, whom they described as "attractive, successful, and happy." Only 2% went for redheads; most describing redheaded men as "good, but effeminate, timid and weak."

If you dislike your hair color, blame your genes. The amount and type of pigment in each hair is largely determined by your genetic code. Two blonde genes gives you blonde hair. Dark hair is the result of two dark-haired genes, or one dominate dark gene combined with a submissive gene (W. Cooper, 1971).

While some men shave their heads intentionally to make a statement, others are grieving the natural loss of their hair. Everybody loses hair on a daily basis. Individual scalp hairs grow for two to six years, take a three-month rest, and then are pushed out by a new hair growing from the same root. The lost of 40 to 60 hairs per day is normal (Hix, 1977). However, the American Medical Association reports that by age 45, about 38% of American males have thinning hair (Duhe, 1988). One might guess that most of the other 62% are worrying about it.

Two common types of baldness are *alopecia prematura* (early baldness) and *alopecia senilis* (old-age baldness). One man in five begins to lose his hair after adolescence and is nearly bald by age 30 (W. Cooper, 1971). Of men who are bald or balding, 78% are self-conscious about their own heads, and 82% are keenly aware of other men's heads, looking for signs of hair loss (Sadick, 1991). Trying to overcome the fact that they are balding, 66% of these men modify their hairstyle. They hope that by wearing what hair they have left in a new way, they can hide the fact that much of it is gone.

About a third of balding men figure if they can no longer grow hair on their scalps, they will grow a mustache or beard. Another third of balding men give up on hair entirely and work on improving their physique (Sadick, 1991).

With all this fuss over hair loss, more than one barber told me that when a balding man comes in for a trim, it is important to soothe his ego by taking longer with his hair than necessary. However, not every man is so concerned about having a hairy dome. One customer joked, "I don't pay the barber to cut my hair, I just hire him to help me find some hair on my head!"

The process of balding is affected by many factors, both

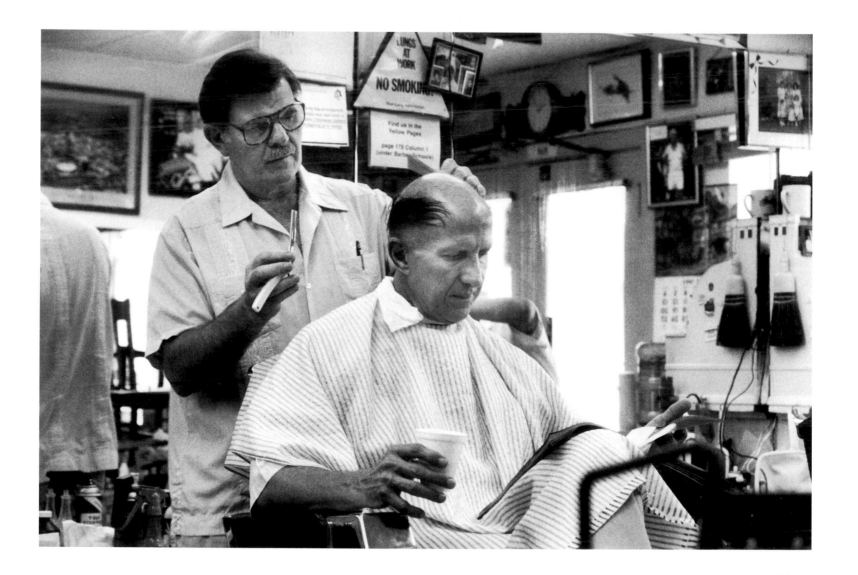

environmental and genetic. Physical exercise promotes hair growth. Men who do manual labor are less likely to go bald then men who have jobs that do not require physical exertion (De Zemler, 1939).

Dr. Young at Howard University found that when he surgically tightened the scalps of monkeys, they developed baldness patterns similar to male pattern baldness (W. Cooper, 1971). Natural baldness is almost unknown in primates other than humans. Perhaps as the human brain evolved larger and larger, the scalp on the top became so thin that the blood does not always flow well enough to supply it with needed nutrients. Hair on the sides of the head is retained because there remains enough fat and muscle to allow proper circulation.

Baldness from poor circulation may also be due to wearing one's tie too tight. Men who wear improperly fitting ties reduce the blood circulation to their head. With more and more men working at desks and wearing ties, can we expect more bald heads in our future? This is more likely to please hat salesmen than barbers.

Doctors Szasz and Robertson at the University of Chicago also endorse the reduced circulation theory of baldness, but identify the cause as smiling. The physical act of smiling and laughing causes the muscles of the face and scalp to tighten, constricting the blood vessels. Perhaps that explains why so many clowns are portrayed as being bald.

Baldness can also be due to hormone production, a product of the testicles. Men who do not develop secondary sex characteristics, or men who lost their testicles in accidents or injuries early in life, do not go bald (W. Cooper, 1971).

Concern over hair loss is not a new concept for men. The Old Testament mentions baldness numerous times. For example, Elisha's baldness is taunted, "He went up from there to Bethel; and while he was going up on the way, some small boys came out of the city and jeered him saying 'Go up, you baldhead! Go up, you baldhead!'" (*4 Kings 2:23*). Most references to baldness are related to grief and stress. "They cast dust on their heads and wallow in ashes; they make themselves bald for you, and gird themselves with sack cloth, and they weep over you in bitterness of soul, with bitter mourning" (*Ezekiel 27:31*); "Son of man, Nebuchadrezzar king of Babylon made his army labor hard against Tyre; every head was made bald and every shoulder was rubbed bare; yet neither he nor his army got anything from Tyre to pay for the labor that he had performed against it" (*Ezekiel 29:18*); and "Make yourselves bald and cut off your hair for the children of your delight; make yourself as bald as the eagle, for they shall go from you into exile" (*Micah 1:16*).

From the Vedas, a holy writing from India, we know that Hindus were paying attention to their hair in 1000 B.C. because they recorded formulas for hair tonics. If you are balding, you may note some of the remarkable potions suggested throughout the ages. Perhaps the earliest recipe is credited to the mother of King Chata of Egypt in 4000 B.C. It called for rubbing the scalp with ground dog's paw, dates, and asses' hooves which had been cooked in oil. The Greek Hippocrates, known as the "father of medicine," was mixing

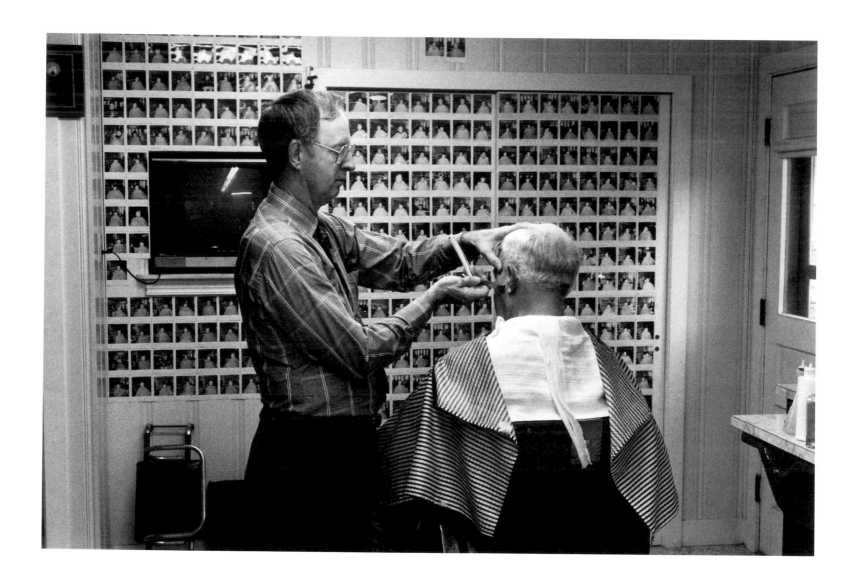

potions in 400 B.C. to produce a tonic to prevent hair loss (De Zemler, 1939). He used a mixture containing essence of roses and lilies, the oil from unripe olives, pigeon droppings, crushed horseradish, beetroot, and nettles. He combined all this with opium. With that prescription, even if the patient's hair was not restored he would be too high to care.

About the same time the Romans were keeping their baldness treatments simple. Just use myrrh berries to prevent baldness in the first place. If that failed ("Maybe you didn't use enough of them?"), then rub the head with bear's fat to restore the hair.

The 16th century brought an exotic elixir assembled by Paracelsus, alchemist and physician, of blood shed in childbirth, blood of a newly-born baby, and the secret ingredient, "vipers' wine." The 16th-century text, *Natural Magick*, by Giovanni Battista della Porta, advised combining the ashes of a hedgehog, burnt bee or flies, and man's burnt dung, all in a honey base. For more rapid results, he suggested marsh mallow root with hog's grease, boiled in wine. For the really impatient, he insisted that burned barley bread, horse fat, and boiled river eel was the way to go.

As science (or quackery) advanced into the 17th century, a chemist in Naples, Josefo Francipolli, produced "Vine Dew," "Calf Water," and "Octopus Fat." His three products could be applied externally or drunk, and promised to cure "falling hair." Although all three consisted primarily of river water, he must have been doing something right; he enjoyed brisk sales until he was killed, at the age of 74, with a full head of hair, in a duel over a lover.

In the 1800s, Dr. Brown-Sequart concocted a lotion of fluid from the sexual glands of monkeys and human female urine (W. Cooper, 1971).

Today, baldness is still big business. Approximately 1.5 million men miss their hair so much that they purchase and wear someone else's hair in the form of a toupee. In one year alone, nearly 42,000 hair-transplant procedures were performed in the U.S. (Sadick, 1991).

However, the best cure is attributed to Drew Berkowitz, who simply stated, "Hair: the only thing that will really prevent baldness."

Human fascination with hair continues even after death. Many people, particularly young boys who read horror comic books, believe that the hair of a dead person continues to grow in the grave. Biologist M. Ryder (1973) points out that although this is technically correct, it is wildly exaggerated:

> Although it is true that not all parts of an organism die at the same time, since some tissues can go on living longer than others, it is unlikely that hair can grow for more than a few minutes after death (and then imperceptibly); indeed, only until the division of any cells undergoing mitosis is complete. The legend that hair can grow after death may have arisen from the observation that shrinkage of the skin following death causes a greater length of hair—on a man's chin for example—to become visible above the surface.

After noting so much fervor and fanaticism on the subject of follicles and their styling, I think the final word on hair I will leave to Wendy Cooper from her book, *Hair: Sex, Society, Symbolism*:

> So much feeling and so much indignation over the centuries about little bits of hair on the face or the length of the hair on the head! It is impossible not to feel that all that energy might have been better employed fighting the very real injustices and abuse of the times.

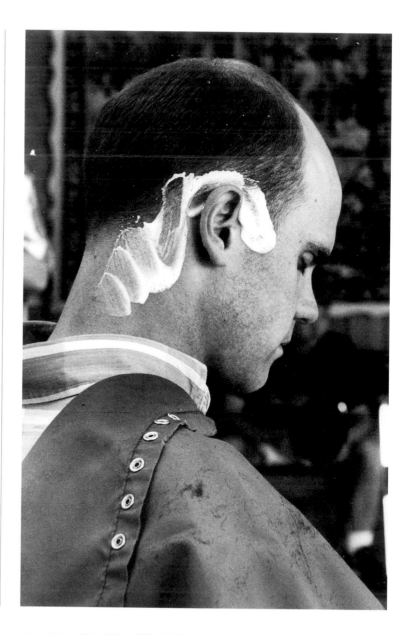

CHAPTER NINE

On Beards and Shaving

> Most men should not wear facial hair of any kind, particularly beards.... the only men who should wear it are those men who must compensate for some other weakness in their appearance or personality.
>
> —*John Molloy,*
> *Dress for Success (1988)*

> A beard is the traditional badge of the leader, the prophet, and the philosopher.
>
> —*Wendy Cooper,*
> *Hair: Sex, Society, Symbolism (1971)*

Shaving and barbers used to be synonymous. In fact, the very term barber comes from the Latin, *barba*, which means beard. Nowadays, we forget that every man has a beard. Webster gives two definitions of beard: "(a) the hair that grows on the chin and cheeks and around the lips, especially of a man; hence a mark of virility; (b) this hair ... when worn long or trimmed in various shapes." Most people just think of the second definition—a permanent beard—and forget that every man has a beard. Some are just made short by daily shaving to the point of being nearly invisible.

On the average, a man's beard covers one third of a square foot, and consists of about 15,500 whiskers. Each whisker grows at the rate of fifteen 1,000ths of an inch every day, and is nearly as strong as a copper wire of the same diameter (Blount, 1986). It is hard to believe that this minuscule daily growth could feel so rough at the end of a day when a man rubs his face against somebody he is hugging or kissing—but generations of children will attest to this fact.

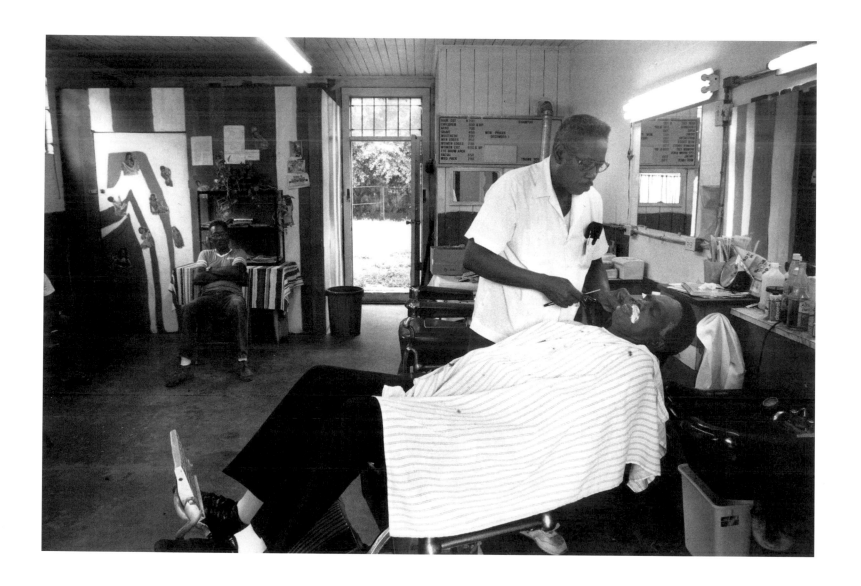

Facial hair has a slightly different chemical composition than scalp hair; this is why whiskers and scalp hair on the same person can differ in color (De Zemler, 1939).

Throughout history, numerous philosophers and authors (including yours truly) have held that a beard justifies, in Charles De Zemler's words, "any amount of time and effort spent in caring for it because it helped its wearer to acquire and retain manliness and courage" (1939). Of course, we men hope that women also appreciate a full beard. In *The Arabian Nights*, a young woman reflects, "a tree is only beautiful when it has leaves, and a cucumber only savory when it is coarse and pimpled on the outside. Is there anything more ugly in the world than a man beardless and bald as an artichoke?" (W. Cooper, 1971).

Beards and sexuality are intertwined, probably because facial hairs first appear at puberty when a male's interest in sexual behavior is so strong. The relationship between the beard and sexuality is more than psychological or cultural; it is also physical. A man's beard grows more rapidly during periods when he is actively having sexual intercourse than when he is celibate (*Nature*, May 1970).

The ancient Romans regarded shaving as effeminate, until converted by the Greeks who paid a great deal of attention to beards and shaving. The Romans followed the Greek tradition of honoring a man's first shave with an offering of the shaved hair to the gods, followed by a celebration (De Zemler, 1939). Only free men were allowed to be clean shaven. Slaves were required to wear beards (Trusty, 1960).

Facial hair has been the subject of religious teachings and admonitions throughout history. For those in the Jewish faith, shaving the beard was a traditional sign of deep grieving (Andrews, 1904). Moses and other great prophets of the Old Testament were known for their majestic beards, a symbol of patriarchal power. The visionary Ezekiel was told to take a sharp knife to his hair and beard, then to divide the hair into thirds to burn, cut into pieces, and cast about; out of this "shall come forth a fire into all the house of Israel (*Ezekiel 5:1–4*).

In ancient Israel, haircutting of all sorts was strictly avoided during religious festivals, a time of holiness. This became ingrained in custom and folklore, as in the old English rhyme:

It was better you were never born
Than on the Sabbath pare hair or horn.

In 1592, barbers could be severely fined if caught giving a shave on Sunday (W. Cooper, 1971).

The early Christian writer Tertullian denounced shaving as blasphemy (De Zemler, 1939). I suppose he figured if God had wanted men to have a naked face, he wouldn't have created beards. The Vatican in 1583 required that priests shave their upper lip so that, when they took holy communion, the wine and wafer which they believed transformed into the blood and body of Jesus would not be contaminated by particles left in the priest's mustache.

The first Pope to wear his beard long was Julius II, who ascended the throne in 1503; he stated his beard was used to

"inspire the greater respect among the faithful" (Andrews, 1904). Perhaps this is linked to a common image of God as a heavenly father with a great flowing beard. Ironically, the devil is usually portrayed with a beard as well—but rather than a long full beard, Satan seems to prefer a neatly trimmed style. This image was so ingrained that the author of *Dress for Success* stated, "People do not trust or believe men in goatees; perhaps it's the devil image" (Molloy, 1988).

Alexander the Great had a practical reason for shaving. He ordered his Macedonian soldiers to shave their beards so the enemy could not grab facial hair as handles in hand-to-hand combat. The ancient Greek soldiers also adopted this style (Andrews, 1904). They determined it was a lesser risk to cut your own face shaving in the morning than to chance having someone else cut your entire head off later in the day.

Shakespeare aired strong views on facial hair in *Much Ado About Nothing*, as Beatrice states, "Lord! I could not endure a husband with a beard on his face; I had rather lie in the woollen." But in the next breath, she states, "He that hath a beard is more than a youth, and he that hath no beard is less than a man."

During Shakespeare's time and the reign of Queen Elizabeth, a man's profession often determined how his beard was trimmed—hence the phrase, "By their beards ye shall know them." Soldiers wore their beards in a pointed sword-shaped fashion. Churchmen wore the "cathedral beard" which mimicked the stone abutments common on the sides of churches at that time. In 1583, any barber worth his snuff knew how to cut and trim the following beard styles: sugar-loaf, forked, spade, swallow-tail, bush, stiletto, needle, Roman T., French, Dutch, Spanish, Italian, screw, fantail, common, court, country, gentlemen's, mean, and bravado. He would also have been skilled in the art of beard waxing, oiling, powdering, and braiding (W. Cooper, 1971).

Certain political leaders attempted to raise funds by taxing facial hair. In 1705, Peter the Great in Russia imposed a beard and mustache tax. It ranged from 30 to 100 rubles per year (Andrews, 1904). The rate of taxation varied according to the social rank of the individual. The twist was, unlike taxes in America, the wealthier the individual, the *more* tax he paid. The idea of the tax was reportedly not only to raise funds, but also to discourage the wearing of beards. To drive the point home, Peter was known to gleefully pluck out, or shave with a dull razor, the beards of repeat offenders (Krumholz, 1992).

Sociologist Dwight Robinson (1976) suggested an important reason for facial-hair changes throughout history. He noted that hairstyles used by each new generation of men generally exhibit certain traits distinct from the hairstyles of the previous generation. "As long as any considerable number of people who have stuck to a superseded form of personal appearance are still living, the young may tend to avoid such a style as old hat. These distasteful associations seem to be safely overcome only after the passage of a century or more." Robinson studied more than a century of male hairstyles shown in drawings and photographs which appeared in the *London Illustrated News* from 1842 to 1972. He noted that any given style faced "nearly complete dor-

mancy" for a specific period of time after it fell from fashion.

Robinson carefully calculated peaks of popularity and cycles for various whisker types. For instance, he noted a 70-year cycle for wearing sideburns with a mustache. Beards or mustaches alone came into fashion every 120 years or so. Mustaches alone climaxed between 1917 and 1919, while beards had their heyday in 1892. Sideburns as a solo act were at their hottest in 1853. (However, if his cycles were correct, then sideburns should have been a fad again in 1993.)

In America, long beards were in fashion for national leaders throughout much of the 19th century. We think of Abraham Lincoln with his distinctive chin whiskers. It was said that he shaved his upper lip while allowing the rest of his beard to grow because he found it messy to eat soup with a mustache (De Zemler, 1939). Theodore "Teddy" Roosevelt is remembered with his walrus mustache. Civil War paintings and photographs show Ulysses S. Grant with a full, trimmed beard, which he kept when he made it to the White House. Presidents Hayes, Harrison, and Garfield had long beards. Cleveland and Taft had mustaches. President Arthur wore a mustache and long sideburns.

More recently, not being clean shaven has often been viewed as being anti-establishment or radical. In *Dress for Success*, this warning is given to those who want "A twentieth century approach":

> Most men should not wear facial hair of any kind, particularly beards. The response to facial hair is almost always negative in corporate situations, and the only men who should wear it are those men who must compensate for some other weakness in their appearance or personality. [Molloy, 1988]

Musicians, artists, philosophers, and psychiatrists (particularly Freudians) seem to be the only ones who can wear their beards long without being thought of as troublemakers. However, if Webster was right and facial hair is a sign of virility (i.e. "strength, vigor, and forcefulness"), then I say it is time to elect a hairy president. Right now we have too many clean-shaven men running for our country's highest office who are more concerned with re-election than leadership.

Let's vote in a bearded congress, too, while we're at it, and get this country back on track. I'm sure Teddy Roosevelt would say "Bully!" to that.

Shaving with a straight-razor is one of the artforms of the barbershop. To the outsider, it can appear downright dangerous. Consider the following story of the apprentice barber in England:

> The duke entered the barber shop in Bardard Castle and asked for the master barber. The fourteen-year-old apprentice reported that he was unavailable. Upon hearing this the duke asked the boy if he could shave. "Yes sir, I always do," was the reply. "But can you shave without cutting?" "Yes, sir, I'll try," answered the youth. "Very well," said the duke, while seating himself and loading his pistol;

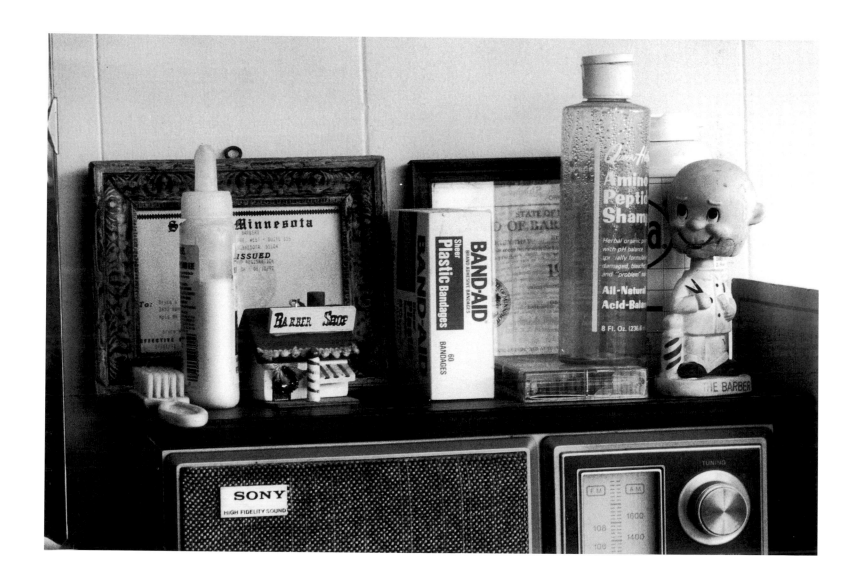

"but look here, if you let any blood, as sure as I sit here I'll blow your brains out! Now consider well before you begin." After a moment's reflection, the boy began to make ready and said, "I'm not afraid of cutting you, sir," and in a short time had completed the feat without a scratch to the complete satisfaction of the duke. In gentle tones his grace asked, "Were you not afraid of having your brains blown out, when you might have cut me so easily?" "No sir, not at all; because I thought that as soon as I should happen to let any blood, before you could have time to fire I would have cut your throat." It need scarcely be added that the duke never resumed his dangerous threats in a barber shop. [Andrews, 1904]

Commodus, Roman emperor from 180–192 A.D., was so impressed by the art of shaving that he would rent a barber-shop, invite his friends over, and shave them (De Zemler, 1939). The first known text on shaving was *Pogonotomy. The Art of Learning to Shave Oneself*, published in France in 1769 by Jean-Jacques Perret (Krumholz, 1992). If you have never before heard the term *pogonotomy*, it may be because the author created it to give his book a more impressive title. It never caught on.

The *Standardized Textbook of Barbering* (A.M.B.A., 1931) describes fourteen separate movements used in giving a shave. These do not include blade stropping, or the proper placing of the steam towel (described in a separate section). In addition, there are four hand positions to be learned: the free hand, the back hand, the reverse free hand, and the reverse back hand.

When purchasing a shave from a barber, most men had a once-over shave because it was cheaper. However, on special occasions—such as a likelihood of an intimate face-to-face encounter with a young lady—he might spring for a twice-over shave to get that soft-as-a-baby's-behind effect. The modern twin-blade shaving systems seek to create the same effect. A close shaving technique popular in the Middle Ages in Europe was called "spoon shaving." Barbers inserted their thumbs into customers' mouths in order to stretch the skin and eliminate wrinkles to facilitate a better shaving. For an additional charge, a spoon was used; this provided an even cleaner shave than the barber's digit. It was so superior that the price for a spoon shave was 33% greater than a thumb shave (De Zemler, 1939).

Most men today do not take time to savor a shave, but merely give themselves a once-over with an electric razor, or slap on some shaving foam and drag a blade over their faces. Having someone shave you is an experience in luxury. The chair is reclined. A hot, moist towel is placed on the face to soften the beard and skin. As that towel is having its relaxing effect, a second towel is prepared. The barber tests the temperature of the hot towel by placing it on the inside of his arm. He then applies the shaving foam. The best motion for applying shaving foam with a brush is to move the brush up and down; circular motion tends to weaken the bristles. The best shaving brushes are made of English badger hair, because the bristles do not stick together when wet (Graeber, 1990).

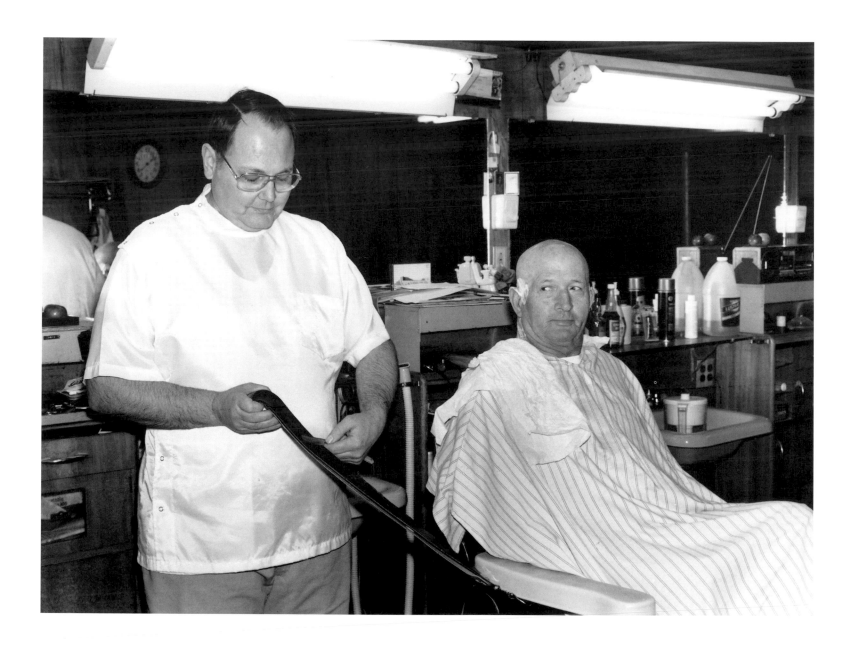

A traditional barber chair is designed to make shaving easy for both the barber and the customer. The chair reclines fully so that the customer lies nearly flat. His head is supported by the headrest, and his feet rest atop the upholstered side of the footrest. You may notice that a traditional barber chair has a footrest with two usable sides. The metal side is used when the customer is sitting upright, with his shoes flat on the footrest. When he reclines for a shave, the footrest is flipped and the customer places his ankles or calves on the soft upholstered side, which is more comfortable and keeps his pants clean.

Of course some men are opposed to being pampered, as you can see from this *Saint Paul Daily* newspaper article, circa 1932:

> America is a nation of tender faces, Erich Lingsfeld, a barber who has just come here from Germany, has found. Faces here are made tender by too much coddling with hot towels and cream & all the other frills that American barbers use, Mr. Lingsfeld declares. In Germany he explains, the barber just lathers up the customer's face, shaves it, and then leaves him to wash it off himself. And there are no soft barber chairs either.

Maybe if German men in the 1930s and '40s had gotten better shaves, they would not have been in such a hurry to march off to a second world war.

If Gerry Harley or Denny Rowe are any indication, the British are not overly fond of the leisurely shave any more than the Germans. These two gentlemen are the fastest shaving barbers in the world, according to *The Guinness Book of Records* (1992). In 1984, Mr. Harley used a straight razor to shave 235 men, averaging 15.3 seconds per face. He drew blood only once, and there were no casualties. Four years later, Mr. Rowe also spent an hour shaving one man after another. He used a safety razor to whack away at an incredible 1,994 beards! Although he averaged but 1.8 seconds per volunteer, he caused blood to flow only four times.

In my view, getting a shave or a haircut is supposed to be a soothing experience, not a race against time. I am thankful that there are still those who agree with me. In one barbershop I visited, there was a button on the wall that the barber pushed when a customer entered. The button set off a buzzer in the saloon next door. A moment later, the bartender entered the shop with a freshly-drawn mug of beer for the customer to enjoy while waiting his turn for the barber's chair. The cost of the brew was added to the price of the trim.

Such service, though harder to find today, has been available for centuries. Consider, for example, this description of Italian barbers given in 1330 by a Dominican monk:

> Without exception, he is clad in black. He wears a cloak and comes to the customer's house, assisted by a *famulus* [assistant], who carries two silver shaving bowls in a silk bag, a mirror, bottle and container filled with rose essence, soap and pomades. The barber bows several times when approaching the customer, who is then given a silk apron, richly embroidered, and a silk napkin to be fas-

tened around the throat. As soon as the razor has glided over the face in the first stroke, the work is interrupted and the barber repeats the bows. In changing from one side to the other, the barber moves to the back of the customer. During the entire procedure, the assistant holds the mirror steadily and changes his position to enable the customer to have full view of himself at all times. The fee is astoundingly small. [De Zemler, 1939]

A pomade, by the way, is a perfumed dressing for the hair or an ointment for the scalp. Now that is my idea of service. I think a wee bit of coddling once in a while is desirable. However, with the decline of the traditional barbershop, there may come a time when you will be unable to obtain a shave. As one barber told me sadly, "Once you stop doing shaves, you lose the feel of a man's face. Then when you do give a shave, you do a bad job and then the customer doesn't want another one."

My suggestion: this year you find a barber who still knows how to use a razor and get a proper shave. It is something every man ought to experience at least once in his life. If I had a son, when it came time for him to shave for the first time, I would offer to take him out for breakfast and then to the barber for a shave.

I would learn from the ancient Greeks and Romans to make his first shave a celebration of manhood.

CHAPTER TEN

A Brief History of Barbering

The trades altogether are like a necklace, and the barber is the chief pearl of the string: He excelleth all that are endowed with skill, and under his hand are the heads of Kings.

—*The Arabian Nights*

Barbers have been around a long time. Barbering tools have been found that date from the Neolithic Age, or as it is more affectionately known, the Stone Age (De Zemler, 1939). This is the period of time, circa 10,000 years ago, when humans were just developing polished stone weapons and other tools. There are prehistoric drawings on the walls of caves showing beardless men, as well as men with short beards. Stone blades were used to trim the hair, crude tweezers have been found that may have been used to pluck the hair, and many cultures used burning twigs to singe the hair rather than cutting it (Krumholz, 1992). The trimming of hair was not merely for the sake of vanity. Long hair was dangerous. It provided one's enemy with a hand-hold during combat, and made a wonderful breeding ground for lice, fleas, and other freeloaders.

The Egyptians, always the innovators, had haircare tools in 4,000 B.C. Their pyramids contained not only tools but hieroglyphics describing their use—sort of the earliest-known owner's manual. With lots of time on their hands,

the royalty shaved their entire bodies, but then wore artificial beards to be more god-like since they assumed the gods did not shave (Krumholz, 1992).

The Greeks had barbers by 500 B.C. It took Romans citizens till around 296 B.C. to appreciate the skills of barbers. However, the legions of Roman soldiers remained unconverted; they sanded their beards off with pumice stones. The Babylonians took their beards seriously enough that no oath was binding unless it was sworn upon one's whiskers (Krumholz, 1992). Around 200 B.C., Scipio Africanus (the conqueror of Hannibal) was making a name for himself by shaving daily. Most everyone else took to the blade once a month or so.

In the 10th century, Arab street barbers wandered about wearing belts with hooks from which dangled the tools of the trade. As one of these early barbers strode down the road, the sound of his razor, scissors, mirror, water bottle, honing stone, and basin clanking together announced his arrival—much like the bell of the old-fashioned ice-cream truck centuries later. The customer merely squatted at the side of the road or made use of a nearby rock or stump (De Zemler, 1939).

Many early peoples believed that hair clippings had the power to bewitch because evil spirits could enter the body through the hair on the head. This vulnerability could be reduced by keeping the hair shortly cropped. Since hair possessed such power, the privilege of cutting it was reserved for the medicine man or priest of the tribe (Trusty, 1960). Thus a single individual served at once as barber, surgeon, dentist, and clergy. Long hair was thought to be particularly powerful. It was this belief that led Roman judges to order the hair of Christian martyrs cut prior to having them put to death.

As the base of human knowledge grew, people began to specialize. Those who studied to be clergy used their skills to heal the sick by prayer, assisted by barber-surgeons who performed blood-letting by cutting the patient or using leeches. This partnership ended in 1163 A.D., when the Catholic Church decided it was sacrilegious for the clergy to be involved in anything that involved human blood (Trusty, 1960).

The combined services of haircare and surgery continued long after this. The two fields were so intertwined that when one referred to someone as a barber, it was understood to be short for barber-surgeon. The Company of Barbers-Surgeons was incorporated by King Henry VIII in 1541. The organization was founded largely to cope with the competition from blacksmiths, who were also offering surgery as a sideline! Eventually, by laws were written which decreed, among other things, that "No decrepit, diseased or deformed apprentice shall be retained by a barber; No barber is to use more than one shop and; No person is to show his porringers [small metal vessels], saucer or basins with blood therein." In addition, Sunday was set aside as a day of rest.

Despite all efforts, squabbles over various matters led Parliament and King George to separate barbers and surgeons into two corporations in 1745. Those who went with the surgeons' group were restricted to blood-letting, tooth-pulling, and use of herbal treatments. They continued their

squabbling and eventually divided again into surgeons and dentists, although some time later. The last known man to practice the trade of barber-surgeon was Mr. Middleditch of London who died in 1826 (J.B.H.C., 1934).

When barbers had stopped wandering the streets plying their trade and settled into shops, it did not take long for these shops to become vital social gathering places. Prior to the invention of printing presses and broadcast media, the barbershop was a news center of the town. Barbershops were so well known as clearinghouses of news that when a person disclosed a stale tidbit of gossip, people would respond, "Every barber knows that!"

Reflecting the social importance of these centers, numerous classical composers used barbershops as settings for their operas. The composers Cornelius (*Barber of Baghdad*), Hallah (*The Barbers of Bassurah*), Leoncavallo (*The Youth of Figaro*), Mozart (*Marriage of Figaro*), and Rossini (*The Barber of Seville*) all wrote musical tales of barbers (De Zemler, 1939). Figaro, the barber in *The Barber of Seville,* makes his stage entrance with a guitar suspended from his neck as he sings:

I'm the factotum [agent] of all the town, make way! Quick now to business, morning hath shown, 'tis day.

Oh, 'tis a charming life, brimful of pleasure, that of a barber, used to high life!

Early and late, for all who require me, nothing can tire me, ready for all.

Of all professions that can be mentioned, that of a barber is best of them all.

Scissors in hand, 'mongst my combs and my razors, I stand at the door, when customers call.

I am in such request, nor night nor day I've rest.

I'm indispensable, irreprehensible, I'm the factotum of all the town!

[translation by Fred Rullman, Inc., New York, 1985]

When Warner Brothers Looney Tunes did a satire of *The Barber of Seville*, they titled it *The Bunny of Seville,* and cast none other than Bugs Bunny himself in the lead role. The cotton-tailed barber accosts his reluctant customer, Elmer Fudd, and begins to sing:

How do? Welcome to my shop. Let me cut your mop, let me shave your crop, daintily, daintily.

Hey you, don't look so perplexed. Why must you be vexed? Can't you see you're next? Yes, you're next.

How about a nice close shave? Teach your whiskers to behave with lots of lather, lots of soap. Don't be a dope.

Now we're ready for the scraping. There's no use to try escaping. Yell and scream and rant and rave. It's no use you need a shave.

There, you're nice and clean. Although your face looks like it might have gone through a machine.

[Warner Brothers, 1991]

Since the rich had slaves or valets to shave them, barbershops gained a reputation for being gathering places for loungers and newsmongers who did nothing less than

gossip, tell smutty stories, and generally scandalize decent folks (Trusty, 1960; and J.B.H.C., 1934). Although some saw barbershops as seedy places, barbers themselves were generally viewed with affection. In 1904, English author William Andrews described the barber's congeniality in his book, *At the Sign of the Barber Pole*:

> The old-fashioned barber has passed away. In years agone (sic) he was a notable tradesman, and was a many-sided man of business, for he shaved, cut hair, made wigs, bled, dressed wounds, and performed other offices. When the daily papers were not in the hands of the people he retailed the current news, and usually managed to scent the latest scandal, which he was not slow to make known—in confidence, and in an undertone, of course. He was an intelligent fellow, with wit as keen as his razor; urbane, and having the best of tempers. It has been truthfully said of this old-time tradesman that one might travel from pole to pole and never encounter an ill-natured or stupid barber.

Andrews and other authors also mentioned the presence of women barbers in London, including the "five women barbers of Drury Lane" in the era of Charles II (W. Cooper, 1971).

Barbers have long been an organized lot. The first recorded barber association was set up in France in 1252 A.D., creating a code of rules and regulations for its members (De Zemler, 1939). Not to be outdone, 56 years later the English set up the Worshipful Company of Barbers. It served both as a social club and to set standards to regulate the craft (Krumholz, 1989). The first English master barber was Richard le Barbour, who obtained this rank in the year 1308 A.D. (J.B.H.C., 1934). It was his responsibility to reprimand any barber he found in London who was acting in a manner to bring disgrace on the guild—such as taking part in some other trade less reputable than barbering. In 1461, the English Barbers Guild was granted a charter by King Edward IV. One of the perks awarded to the Barbers Guild—in contrast to lesser associations serving musicians, singers, actors, dog-catchers, grave-diggers, and executioners—was the right to carry a sword in public (De Zemler, 1939).

American barbers organized some four hundred years later. Dutch and Swedish settlers are recorded as being the first professional barbers in America. On the east coast, men of wealth and status were clean shaven, had trimmed hair, and often wore wigs. In those days, most wig wearers shaved their heads in order to accommodate a more comfortable fitting wig. One reason wigs were popular was that syphilis was widespread, and sufferers experienced hair loss as a symptom. On the frontier, men let their scalp hair and beards grow. In many parts of the country, slaves brought from Africa were used as barbers, leading to a decline in the prestige of the trade for Caucasians. It was not until after the Civil War, when waves of French, English, German, and Italian immigrants landed—and many opened barbershops—that Caucasians again began to view barbering as an attractive social position (Trusty, 1960).

The first significant organizational move for barbers in

America was the founding convention in 1887 of the Journeymen Barbers' Union, held in Buffalo, New York, on November 5th. By 1919, it would have 41,032 members. By 1929, 51,879 men were enrolled. In 1888, the Union succeed in reducing the work week from 90 to 70 hours.

Once barbers organized, they made agreements with other trade organizations for mutual support. In 1887, the American Federation of Labor asked its members to stop patronizing any barbershop that charged less that three cents for a shave and ten cents for a haircut, so barbers could make a decent wage.

In 1893, A.B. Moler opened the first American barber school, "out west" in Chicago. That same year, the first journal of barbering was printed. Soon afterwards, Minnesota got into the act. Their state legislature passed the first American barber license law in 1897. This lead to an avalanche of similar laws in most other states (Table 2). California, Kansas, Kentucky, Nebraska, and New York actually repealed their laws at various points in time, only to re-enact them later.

By 1930, the State Boards of Barber Examiners and other barber organizations agreed upon a model licensing law, and many states based their statutes on this. These laws were designed to promote the health and welfare of the public by protecting them from persons claiming to understand the science and art of barbering without first obtaining proper training. The laws also specified sanitary practices to prevent the spread of disease.

As the germ theory of disease became widely accepted, the time was ripe for newspapers to publish features on the dangers found in the neighborhood barbershop. As one writer warned, "Baldness is now known to be the aftermath of a really serious disease, commonly transmitted by the barber's hairbrush and only too often the forerunner of a wide range of skin diseases, including cancer" (Krumholz, 1992). In a 1905 article, Dr. Isadore Dyer, M.D., a professor on diseases of the skin, warned other physicians about the dangers of barbershops. The good doctor wrote:

Here are some facts which are well known to every medical man who especially deals with skin diseases: 1) Fully 90% of baldness owes its origin to the barber shop, directly or indirectly. 2) From 10% to 25% of the practice of a specialist in skin diseases comes from barber shop infections and their consequences. 3) The list of skin affections arising from the barber shop includes some of the worst, and among parasitic diseases there are a large number which the usual barber shop practice may spread.

Dr. Dyer went on to cite syphilis, ringworm, "Indian Fire" (Impetigo Contagiosa), lice, lupus (erosion of the skin), herpes, molluscum (rounded tumors), and blastomycosis (a chronic respiratory infection) as dangers lurking in the barber's razor and comb. The article concluded with, "The barber shop is a necessary evil of civilization—largely because men wear short hair and are either too lazy to shave or find the barber less severe than themselves."

One barber told me that in the old days, the two best

places to get a disease were "a barbershop and a whore house." One facial towel for every ten or twelve customers was standard practice at the time. After state laws were passed, barbers were required to wash their hands before attending any patron; to use powdered—rather than stick form—astringent to stop the flow of blood from cuts; to stop using powder puffs and sponges; to wash mugs and shaving brushes between use; to boil or place in a germicide all combs, razors, clippers, and scissors; to sweep the shop floor daily; and to use a towel on only one customer and then to wash it (Krumholz, 1992).

Basically, all the laws passed at this time contained these components:

1. Anyone calling himself a barber must be licensed.
2. To obtain a license, a specific number of hours of training in a barber school and then an apprenticeship must be completed.
3. Once licensed, a barber must work within a licensed barbershop and follow a sanitation code.
4. The governor of the State will appoint a Barber Board to inspect all shops.
5. A copy of the rules must be posted in every shop.
   [Trusty, 1960; and Krumholz, 1992]

Table 2
Early Barber Legislation by State

1897	Minnesota
1899	Missouri, Michigan, Nebraska, and Oregon
1901	California, Connecticut, Delaware, North Dakota, and Washington
1902	Kentucky
1903	Kansas, New York, Rhode Island, Utah, and Wisconsin
1904	Maryland
1907	Texas
1909	Colorado and Illinois
1914	Georgia
1927	South Dakota, Idaho, and Iowa
1928	Louisiana
1929	Arizona, Montana, Nevada, North Carolina, and Tennessee
1930	Mississippi
1931	Alabama, Florida, Massachusetts, New Mexico, Pennsylvania, Oklahoma, and Wyoming
1933	Indiana, New Jersey, and Ohio
1934	West Virginia

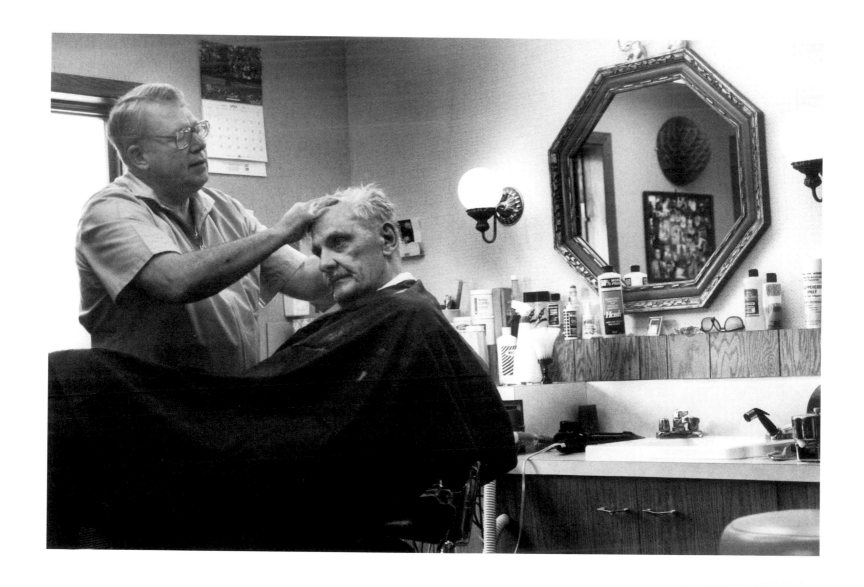

Ever since 1745 in England, when haircutting and surgery became separate occupations, barbers have striven to ensure they are viewed with respect. In 1930, when the U.S. Census classified barbers in the same category as "charwomen, bellhops, and bartenders," C.W. Ward, a barber from Edeley, North Dakota, was outraged. He thought that "the barber is in a different class," and wrote a letter of protest (*Krank's Review*, October 1930). Ward's letter asked, "Is the Census Bureau unaware that barbering is an institute inseparable from civilized life?" He went on to point out that the prophet Ezekiel said, "And thou, son of man, take thee a barber's razor and cause it to pass upon thine head and upon thine beard." Mr. Ward found no Biblical references to charwomen, bellhops, or bartenders.

Until the end of the 19th century, barbering was taught by the apprenticeship method. Even when formal schooling became available, the only entrance requirement was having tuition money. The length of study varied from a few days to several months. Eventually, to become a journeyman barber, you were required to attend an approved school for 1,000 to 1,800 hours of formal study, plus undertake a one- to two-year apprenticeship. By 1924, the Associated Master Barbers of America was formed to raise the standards of the occupation. An Educational Council worked to standardize training among 50 barber schools in operation, developing a curriculum and an approved text book (A.M.B.A., 1931).

Perhaps as a result of once being associated with surgery, barber training has gone well beyond how to cut hair. One would think that instructors would focus only on the neck up, since that is where the barber does his work, but the barber studied much more. The foreword to the *Standardized Textbook of Barbering* (A.M.B.A., 1931) reads like an introduction to a medical textbook.

> Barbering became a science when interest shifted to the study of the physical makeup of the human entity and the nature of the environment in which the human being lives. The human body is the most interesting object on earth, and to know it, especially the portion upon which the barber operates, is indispensable to the proper practice of the profession.
>
> Obviously there is more to the complete and intelligent practice of barbering than mere mechanical movements, just as there is more to the human body than what we see on the outside.... The degree of perfection wrought by the barber in rendering his services is dependent on his understanding of the thing on which he works—the human body ... the most complicated and still the most perfect machine in existence.

The book contains chapters on the following: cells, digestion, vitamins, blood circulation, bones of the head, muscles, nervous system, skin, hair, the shedding and regrowth of hair, electricity, light therapy, theory of color vision, physiological effects of ultraviolet and infra-red rays, pharmacology, oils and fats, creams, antiseptics, germicides, disinfectants, soaps, depilatories, cosmetics, skin and scalp ailments, diseases of the sebaceous and sweat glands, hygiene, sanitation, bacteriology, theory of massage, facials, the clay pack, scalp manipulations, treatments for scalp diseases, shampoos, rinses, dandruff treatments, tinting and dying, and ethics.

Current educational requirements to become licensed as a barber vary from state to state (Table 3). Some states require that students entering a program have a high-school diploma, while others require no prior formal education. Most states expect 1,500 hours of schooling. Nebraska has the longest training program; their barbers complete 2,100 hours of schooling.

Once out of school, some barbers are free to set up shop for themselves. Others must complete an apprenticeship in a shop under the direction of an already-licensed barber. California has the longest apprenticeship, a full two years.

Hanging around barbershops for years, I managed to pick up a few informal tips on how to be a successful barber that I can pass on to you:

1. "Don't throw all the cut hair out at night. Save some of it to 'seed' the floor in the morning, so when the first customer comes in it looks like you have already cut someone's hair. Customers are afraid to be the first cut of the day. They worry that you're not fully awake yet and might do a poor job."
2. "Learn to read people. Never act superior to anyone."
3. "Never bad-mouth another barber's work. It is bad for the trade to have barbers insulting each other—makes us look as bad as politicians! Besides that, if the customer liked how the last barber cut his hair, if you insult the haircut you are insulting the customer. Basically telling him he doesn't know a good cut from a bad one."
4. If you want a good haircut yourself: "If you have to go to an unfamiliar shop to get a trim, go to a two-man shop and wait for the chair of the barber with the worse haircut to open up. You'll be assured of getting the better barber—because they cut each other's hair."

Table 3
Educational Requirements to Become a Barber

	Education required (grades)	Barber School hours	Apprenticeship (months)		Education required (grades)	Barber School hours	Apprenticeship (months)
Alabama	No state barber laws			Nebraska	12	2100	0
Alaska	0	1500	9	Nevada	12	1500	18
Arizona	10	1450	18	New Hampshire	12	1500	24
Arkansas	8	1500	18	New Jersey			
California	9	1500	24	New Mexico	0	1200	0
Colorado	0	1250	0	New York	8	1000	18
Connecticut	8	1500	0	North Carolina	0	1528	12
Delaware	8	1500	12	North Dakota	12	1550	15
Florida	0	1200	0	Ohio	8	1800	0
Georgia	9	1500	18	Oklahoma	10	1500	18
Hawaii	0	0	6	Oregon			
Idaho	10	1500	18	Pennsylvania	8	1250	0
Illinois	12	1500	0	Rhode Island	10	1500	24
Indiana	12	1500	0	South Carolina	9	1500	12
Iowa	10	2100	0	South Dakota	10	1500	12
Kansas	12	1500	0	Tennessee	10	1500	0
Kentucky	12	1500	18	Texas	7	1500	0
Louisiana	12	1500	0	Utah			
Maine	10	1500	18	Vermont	12	1500	12
Maryland	0	1200	15	Virginia	0	1500	3000 hours
Massachusetts	0	1000	18	Washington			
Michigan	10	2000	0	Washington D.C.	0	1000	24
Minnesota	10	1500	12	West Virginia	8	2000	0
Mississippi	8	1500	0	Wisconsin			
Missouri	8	1000	0	Wyoming	12	1500	0
Montana	8	2000	0				

Based on information provided by the National Association of Barber Schools (1990).

CHAPTER ELEVEN

Reasons for the Decline in Barbershops

It is pure good-will to my race which leads me to commend the Star [safety] Razor to all who travel by land or by sea, as well as to all who stay at home.

—Oliver Wendell Holmes

The traditional barbershop has been endangered for some time, according to a number of observers, its total numbers rising and falling with the ups and downs of the American economy. As you can see in Table 4, the number of dentists and physicians tended to stay fairly stable in the twenty years from 1919 to 1939, while the number of barbers fluctuated dramatically, with a serious drop during the Great Depression of the 1930s.

Table 4
Number of Barbers, Physicians, and Dentists
Over Twenty Years

Year	Barbers	Physicians	Dentists
1919	182,965	144,977	56,153
1929	261,092	131,675	61,315
1939	82,000	150,000	56,000

[from U.S. census data]

After World War II the number of shops increased again, so that by 1948 there were appropriately 92,000 shops. By 1967, the number had climbed to 112,000. In the 1970s, however, that began to drop sharply.

Between 1972 and 1977 alone, the Bureau of the Census reported that the number of barbershops declined 25%. From 1972 to 1990, a total of 108,168 barbers died, retired, or went into another trade. In those same years, 45,772 barbershops closed forever. According to the National Association of Barber Schools, there were only 62,507 shops left by 1990 (see Table 5 on facing page).

Today, only half of the males in America get their hair cut in a barbershop. The other half have their hair cut at home or go to a unisex hairstylist (Exter, 1990). Unfortunately, when boys of today's generation think of a barber, the image that comes to mind is strange old Floyd from reruns of the Andy Griffith's *Mayberry R.F.D.* television series. Fortunately, the American males who still want to get their hair cut in a traditional barbershop can find one—at least for now.

If you are the impatient sort and want to get a trim quickly, you had best move to Texas where there are more barbershops than any other state: one barber for every 794 heads. Perhaps they should change their motto to "The Barbershop State." Those of you who live in Indiana must have more patience, since you have only 2,628 barbers to service the entire state—the fewest barbers per capita in the Union.

Table 5
Number of Barbers and Shops in 1990 (and 1972)

	# of Barber Shops	# of Barbers	Population	Ratio: Population/ Barber		# of Barber Shops	# of Barbers	Population	Ratio: Population/ Barber
Alabama	No statistics available				New Hampshire	314	509	920,000	1,808
Alaska	•••				New Jersey	•••			
Arizona	950	3,225	3,714,300	1,152	New Mexico	459	1,201	1,241,000	1,033
Arkansas	950	2,100	2,406,000	1,146	New York	4,740	13,385	17,558,072	1,312
California	5,860	18,896	25,857,500	1,368	N. Carolina	2,250	5,125	5,606,000	1,094
Colorado	900	3,360	3,000,000	892	North Dakota	249	497	652,000	1,312
Connecticut	•••				Ohio	3,534	11,148	10,743,946	964
Delaware	250	539	600,000	1,113	Oklahoma	1,400	3,349	2,892,000	864
Florida	2,886	11,661	12,400,000	1,063	Oregon	•••			
Georgia	1,947	4,958	6,104,000	1,231	Pennsylvania	4,105	10,367	11,731,000	1,132
Hawaii	255	880	1,000,000	1,136	Rhode Island	294	987	929,000	941
Idaho	277	774	943,000	1,218	S. Carolina	1,306	3,050	2,932,000	961
Illinois	Not licensed	7,627	11,418,000	1,497	South Dakota	300	460	670,000	1,457
Indiana	Unknown	2,098	5,490,224	2,628	Tennessee	1,700	4,800	4,000,762	833
Iowa	1,250	2,220	2,902,000	1,319	Texas	8,597	21,395	16,991,000	794
Kansas	1,000	1,875	2,363,000	1,260	Utah	•••			
Kentucky	1,500	3,600	3,723,024	1,034	Vermont	No statistics available			
Louisiana	1,700	3,000	4,480,681	1,494	Virginia	1,028	3,460	5,197,000	1,502
Maine	431	804	1,097,000	1,364	Washington	•••			
Maryland	1,064	5,078	4,349,400	952	Washington D.C.	167	689	656,000	952
Massachusetts	2,308	6,156	5,746,441	934	West Virginia	852	1,290	1,875,000	1,453
Michigan	2,452	7,433	9,200,000	1,238	Wisconsin	•••			
Minnesota	1,170	2,933	4,192,973	1,430	Wyoming	151	282	450,000	1,596
Mississippi	1,050	2,200	2,429,000	1,104	Puerto Rico				
Missouri	1,650	3,987	4,917,000	1,233					
Montana	340	800	786,000	983	**Totals**				
Nebraska	650	1,850	1,570,000	849	1990	62,507	180,668	206,559,323	1,143
Nevada	221	629	825,000	1,312	1972	108,279	288,836	206,256,000	713

Based on information provided by the National Association of Barber Schools.
••• No distinction between barbering & cosmetology establishments

Of course, barbershops are changing. Community institutions of all sorts are always in a state of flux, responding to broad changes in society—in turn, this affects the behavior of individuals; this causes the institutions again to respond. Change is nothing new to humankind. Blacksmiths and wheelwright shops used to be common too.

While change in the fabric of society is not new, the *rate* of change has increased dramatically during the decades of the 20th century. There are numerous reasons that traditional barbershops are disappearing today:

1. the popularity of shaving at home;
2. the availability of home haircutting equipment;
3. the widespread use of automobiles;
4. longer hairstyles;
5. a move towards women hairstylists and the unisex shop;
6. the economic advantages of franchise shops; and
7. stagnant prices.

The Popularity of Shaving at Home

Prior to the turn of the century, men who shaved either used straight razors at home to shave or went to a barber. Some barbers shaved so many men in a day that they let the fingernail on one of their little fingers grow long, to scoop out more easily any shaving foam that strayed into customers' ears or nostrils. In the days of the straight razor, shaving at home was often unpleasant. It was difficult to keep a good edge on a razor, the quality and temperature of water was inconsistent, and many shaving soaps were poor and did not make a good lather.

The first guarded razor was invented in 1847 by William Henson in London. In 1877, the Kampfe Brothers of New York invented what we now call the safety razor. They called it the Star, and were granted U.S. Patent No. 228,904. Oliver Wendell Holmes endorsed it, writing, "It is pure good-will to my race which leads me to commend the Star Razor to all who travel by land or by sea, as well as to all who stay at home" (Krumholz, 1992). Despite such sincere praise, it did not gain widespread acceptance until World War I (1914–1918), when American soldiers were issued the new-fangled safety razors. The Gillette Company made millions of "Khaki" U.S. Army-issue shaving kits for the troops "over there" (Krumholz, 1992). When the soldiers returned to the States, they were used to shaving themselves and were allowed to keep their Army-issue razors. The song lyrics, "How ya gonna keep 'em down on the farm, after they've seen Paree?" (Lewis, Young, and Donaldson, 1919), could have been: "How ya gonna keep 'em down at the barbershop, after they've seen the safety razor?"

As the safety razor become more affordable, men began to think, "Why should I pay a barber 25¢ to shave me when I can use a safety razor and do it myself in the privacy of my home?" (Twenty-five cents in 1919 was about $2 in today's funds.) In the 1920s, city governments began to introduce health regulations forbidding the use of a shaving brush or mug on more than one person. Each customer was required to have his own brush and mug at the shop. This additional expense made it even more difficult for the barber shave to compete with the safety-razor shave at home.

By 1936, the American Safety Razor Company and Gillette were producing half of the country's "penny blades," with combined sales of nearly six million dollars (Krumholz, 1992). The safety razor has remained much the same since its invention, with most attention focused on improving the blade rather than the blade handle. Wilkinson introduced a blade coated with polytetrafluoroethylene in 1961, designed to help the blade glide better over the skin. Then, of course, came the ecologically unsound invention of the disposable razor.

Following World War II, the electric razor became widely available, completing the popular shift to home shaving. The first wind-up mechanical shaver had been patented by Willis G. Shockey in 1910; it was followed by several other brands, none of which caught on. The electric-powered razor was invented in the 1930s, but could not gain public acceptance until most people had their homes electrically wired. Today, there are roughly 6 to 7.5 million electric razors sold each year in America (Gales, 1992). However, electric razors have not fully replaced wet shaving.

I do not know if you can judge a man by whether he uses a blade or an electric razor to shave—but if you think you can, you might like to know that former President Ronald Reagan used an electric razor when he was in the White House. Presidents Nixon, Ford, Carter, and Bush were all wet shavers, using a blade and foam (Graeber, 1990).

Perhaps the final blow to barber shaving has been the fear of contracting the A.I.D.S. virus from a cut. Some people fear that sharing a razor is like sharing an I.V. needle, that the metal blade may have traces of infected blood on it. To increase the safety of barber shaves, straight razors with disposable blades are now available. Some barbers I talked with said they only shave men they have known for years. They will not shave a new customer, afraid that if the customer came down with A.I.D.S., he would sue his barber, claiming infection from a shaving cut. Even having used a disposable blade, the barbers fear that attorneys' fees, time away from their shops in court, and bad publicity could destroy their businesses. Others are reluctant to shave customers because they are afraid, as barbers, if they cut themselves they might contract A.I.D.S. One barber commented sadly, "I suppose one day barbers will have to wear masks and rubber gloves the way dentists do now. That's the day I close up. I can't see having a conversation with a man I've known for twenty years through a mask."

Some barbers have become so nervous that they have not only stopped providing full facial shaves, but have even given up the practice of shaving the backs of customers' necks and around their ears. One barber who refuses to give up the blade is Tony Pietrocini in Cleveland, who insists, "Finishing up a haircut with a shave around the ears and neck is like the cherry on a big sundae" (Phillips, 1995).

Some noted how the safety razor weakened the link between the barber, his customer, and the trade of cutlery. One man went so far as to write an editorial (*Krank's Review*, August 1926) titled, "The safety razor as a destroyer," with this dire warning:

124

Where is the human element employed in the production of Safety Razors and Safety Blades? And what will it lead to? It is a serious question and one that the average man seldom thinks about.

Compare this with the production of a Straight Razor. No one but a skilled mechanic can produce such a razor. Each blade is individually handled and treated, it must be hardened, tempered, ground and finished, handles must be made and fitted all of which requires skill and keeps a number of workmen all earning a living.

... He is out of touch with cutlery experts when he uses a Safety. When he uses a regular razor he goes to the barber to get it honed or he goes to his cutler for that purpose, either one is an expert in his line. From them he can obtain another razor or he can have it honed and can get expert advice on how to use it. If he is having shaving troubles he can find out what is wrong. He is advised about supplies best suited to him. He goes to the Barber Shop oftener, will get his hair cut oftener and get such treatments which will make him look neater. All these things would probably never be brought to his notice if he did not use a Straight Razor.

It keeps up a train of trade which is so necessary to the barber and it benefits the patron.

Razor Grinders are getting scarcer each year. It is a good deal like horseshoeing, they are not needed any more. What is going to happen to the barber who needs that razor and cannot get along with a make-shift? What kind of a razor will the barber use after all the old master grinders and cutlers have been eliminated and when the death knell has been rung to this wonderful skill still to be had in isolated places?

Razor grinders disappeared for reasons other than economic. The average grinder in 1870 was paid $480 per year for a 60-hour week (Krumholz, 1992), the equivalent of about $5,750 today (U.S. Dept. of Commerce). Grinders had a short life. Pneumoconioses, grinder's rot or grinder's disease, was caused by the inhaling of dust from the materials used to manufacture razors, including metals, mother of pearl, tortoise shell and bakelite, bone, horn and silicon. The breathing of these particles was a respiratory recipe for bronchitis, emphysema, pneumonia, cancer, and calcicosis. Fortunately for American business, the depression in England and Ireland forced many men to move to the U.S. and accept whatever work was available, even if it cost them several decades of their life and their ability to breathe well.

Some people think the term *safety razor* is a contradiction in terms. Bill Cosby described shaving this way:

I mean sometimes I get up, and I go into the bathroom, and I look at my face in the mirror, and I see little tiny hairs growing out of my face. And I say, "Hmmm, little tiny hairs growing out of my face." I call my wife, "Come here and look at my face." She say, (sic) "What?" I say, "Come here woman, look at my face!" She say, "Yeah! Little tiny hairs growing out of your face!" I get me some lather and I lather up, and I get my razor and shave. Zip, zop, see

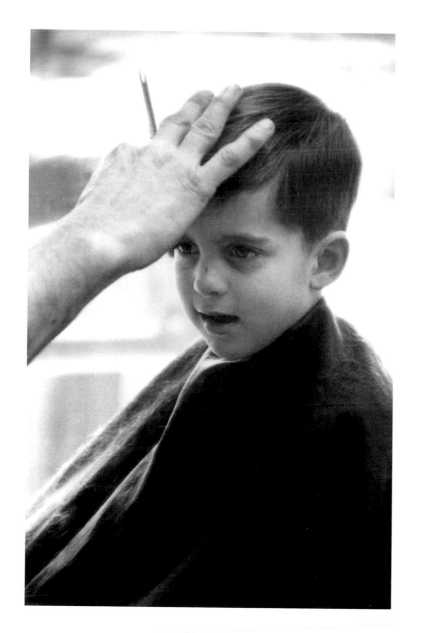

126

that? My face is ripped to sheds. 'Course these razor people go to a lot of trouble to put numbers on this thing. No matter what number you turn to you still cut yourself to pieces. Actually, all I wanted was a clean shave, not a self-sacrifice. [Cosby, no date]

Home Haircutting

The first patent for a hair-clipper for humans was granted in 1879 (*Krank's Review*, August 1925). But it was operated manually, and in the hands of an amateur was not a great improvement over scissors. Most males who could afford it still preferred to get their hair cut by a barber. Home haircutting did not really become popular with the general public until the 1950s, when inexpensive electric hair-clippers became widely available. When I say "popular," cutting hair at home was usually more popular with parents than it was with children.

I remember the day my own mother redeemed her collection of S & H Green Stamps for a home barber kit. The cover of the box showed a happy all-American parent cutting the hair of an equally happy all-American child. The box further assured us that the enclosed clippers would allow "any parent to cut hair with professional results." My parents were enthusiastic, while my brother and I remained skeptical. My parents noted how much money would be saved, and how we kids would no longer *have* to go to the barbershop. I thought a more appropriate phrasing would be: I would no longer *get* to go to the barbershop.

The results were exactly what one would expect when an untrained parent is allowed to wield what is in effect a power tool on their child's head. The sides of my head looked like I had joined the Marines and received a boot-camp haircut. The only part of my appearance which gave me away as a mere civilian were the bangs which hung straight down to my eyebrows.

I was not the only boy who found the home haircutting experience to be, well, not exactly the high point of his childhood. Take, for example, author Frank Wilderson's (1989) boyhood memory:

> "Frank, come into the kitchen!"
>
> A rabbit's foot thumped against my left lung as I sat on a stool before her and imagined my father in the living room groaning on bended knee like a bishop breaking genuflection. Shortly after the sandpaper growl of his slippers on linoleum appeared, tall, gaunt, bleary-eyed and whiskered beneath the kitchen's white trumpets of neon.
>
> "It's time to cut the boy's hair. You should have done it hours ago. He is reciting *Gunga Din* tomorrow in the talent show, or have you forgotten?" ...
>
> My father was quiet during these proceedings, unless I squirmed or cried out or complained too much. Then he'd whack me several times across my thigh and whack me again if I had the audacity to whimper. How could he hear the TV in the living room if I was crying?
>
> The razor dragged swiftly and painfully over my scalp like ... a shovel digging through gravel.

It appears that the home haircutting fad was inexpensive in financial terms, but costly emotionally. As any barber could confirm, there is much more to giving a quality haircut than having a pair of electric clippers.

The Automobile

Urban America used to be organized in small neighborhoods. People did most, if not all, of their activities within the radius of a few miles. They bought their food from the corner grocery. They got their meat from the local butcher. They got their hair cut within walking distance of their home or work. In these small neighborhoods, people had multiple relationships with one another. Your barber was also a member of your church. He was your customer when he came into your store. He might even be related by marriage.

Street-cars and buses expanded the radius of the circle by a few miles, but most people still organized their lives around their neighborhood. However, the introduction of the mass-produced automobile changed American society radically. People began to travel greater distances for goods and services. As the likelihood of multiple relationships diminished, the interactions between customer and service-provider became more superficial.

As early as 1939, people were beginning to notice that barbershops were changing. Barber historian Charles De Zemler was concerned that the friendliness he associated with barbershops was disappearing.

The barber shop today bears little resemblance even to what our grandfathers knew. The atmosphere of a modern barber shop is that of a professional room. It might be a hospital ward, thoroughly sanitary to the smallest detail, streamlined with luxury—or it might be a large dental office. The equipment is planned for efficient personal and individual service. The chair is raised or lowered, moved to right or left by a touch, according to the need of the barber at the moment. A new comb and brush set, thoroughly sterilized, awaits each person. The initialed mugs and the brushes of an older day are gone. The invitation to the chair is cordial but business-like. No time for long-winded discussion in the chair, though talk in a barber shop is just as natural as silence in a mausoleum. The customer sets the mood, not the barber. Overhead is too costly to permit loitering and appointments made ahead often keep the barber on his toes.

Long Hair

Gentlemen used to get their hair cut every two weeks. Even if they did not get "a haircut" they at least got "a trim," having a quarter- to half-inch of hair cut. If a gentleman waited longer than two weeks between visits to his barber, he might well go to another shop to get his hair cut prior to coming back to his regular barber, the customer too embarrassed to let his usual barber see that he had let himself go so long looking unkempt.

This pattern changed in America in the 1960s. By 1967, the British Invasion of musical groups was well underway.

The "mop top" Beatles were heros, playing to sold-out screaming audiences. A year later, the rock musical *Hair* was being performed on Broadway. Male dancers with shoulder-length locks sang proudly about their "curly, fuzzy, shaggy, ratty, matty, shining, gleaming, steaming, knotted, twisted, beaded, braided, powdered, flowered, bangled, tangled, and spangled" hair (Ragni and Rado, 1968). The cast was described as "pro-love, pro-drugs, pro-sex and anti-establishment" (Shapiro, N., 1986, album cover). A person's length of hair was much more than a fashion statement; it was a political statement. "Long said left, short said R.O.T.C." (Hirshev, 1987).

For many of us, the hairstyle of choice was an antistyle. Long hair showed commitment to an ideological statement. The longer the hair, the stronger the commitment (Synnott, 1987). John Weisman (1988) knew that it was politics more than fashion that kept him out of a barber chair for decades. He wrote:

> Barbers represented the System. Lyndon Johnson went to the barber. J. Edgar Hoover went to the barber. Wall Street lawyers and stockbrokers went to the barber. We struggling writers and artists began to see those multi-jointed swivel chairs as yet another manifestation of a society we wanted to change, reform, revolutionize. Radicals didn't want to smell like bay rum or Kreml. A little dab didn't do us.

Only when Weisman turned forty-five—and realized that

being a journalist in Washington covering the White House, Department of State, and network news bureaus qualified him as a member of "the System"—did Weisman return to the smell of witch hazel and his "long-lost youth."

Long hair was viewed as a rejection of the American political system, a violation of gender roles, a lack of support for American troops in Viet Nam, and a sign of using illegal drugs. It naturally caused quite a stir. Those supporting the status quo tried to convince men to get haircuts by warning that long hair was unpatriotic. But to many long-haired men, that was exactly the point. They did not want to be loyal to a country they thought was fighting an unjust war.

Resistance to long hair from those with a more conservative viewpoint was equally impassioned. As late as 1972, the California Unemployment Insurance Appeals Board was still ruling that jobless men with long hair were not eligible for unemployment compensation because of their appearance; they were considered to be voluntarily restricting their availability for employment (Firth, 1973).

Even though fashion magazines of the period were filled with photographs of long hairstyles on women, opponents of long hair on men said long hair was unhealthy because it was not clean. Billboards appeared that read: "Beautify America: Get a haircut."

Disagreements over the length of men's hair predated my high-school days—and my father's comments on my long hair. In 1096 A.D., long-haired men were banned from Catholic churches. Not only that, but when they died, others were not to pray for their souls (De Zemler, 1939). The

debate over the length of men's hair has raged since Biblical times. St. Paul wrote, "Doth not nature itself teach you, that if a man have long hair it is a shame unto him? But if a woman have long hair, it is a glory to her" (*1 Corinthians 11:14–15*). Seems they had double standards back then too. Weren't all those paintings of Jesus with long, flowing locks true to life?

Objections to long hair on men continue to this day. Male employees at Disneyland are fired if their hair is too long, or if they have any form of beard or mustache. *The Disney Look*—a guidebook for the personal appearance of all Disney employees—states:

> Hair: A neat, natural haircut and a clean shave are essential. Hair should be neatly cut and tapered so it does not cover any part of your ears. (Putting your hair behind your ears is not acceptable.) Hair styles termed "natural" or "Afro" are acceptable provided they are neatly packed. [*Harper's Magazine*, June 1990]

I find this prohibition against facial hair ironic since the founder of the organization, Walt Disney, had a full mustache. The hair rules were so strict that some people claimed that at one time you could not be admitted to Disneyland as a *customer* if your hair was too long (Blount, 1986). When I contacted the people at Disneyland, however, they denied they had ever been that strict.

Not everyone has been against long hair on men. One barber told me that, as far as he was concerned, long hair on men was the greatest thing to happen to barbering—besides the invention of electric clippers—because men started to pay more attention to their hair. Prior to this, he often worked on men who "hadn't washed their hair for weeks and had a head full of 'greasy kid stuff.'" He added that, even though cutting long hair was easier than cutting flat-tops, he was able to charge 100% to 150% more for cutting long hair. He noted it is harder to cut short hairstyles properly, because with short hair, as little as 1/32nd of an inch difference between hairs is noticeable. Longer hairstyles allow sloppier work to go undetected.

With long hair, it became fashionable for men to wear their hair tied at the back of the head. The ponytail was a fairly widely-accepted hairstyle for young men in the 1960s, and again in the 1990s. In fact, the ponytail has been in and out of men's fashion for centuries. French King Louis XV started a fashion craze that swept Europe. Men of various classes wore their hair long enough to be done in tresses. It then became the fad to braid the hair, with the queue often encased in a silken bag. Not only did members of the court go for this style, but government officials and military officers joined in as well. In fact, it became part of the official uniform of the Prussian Army (De Zemler, 1939).

Unfortunately, a trend towards longer hairstyles leads to barbers selling fewer haircuts and making less money. It is a simple matter of mathematics. In addition to the financial impact, fewer haircuts means the relationship between the barber and the customer is lessened. There is a social psychological principle, the "mere-exposure effect," that states

that merely being in the *presence* of another person repeatedly leads to the two people liking each other. If the long-haired customer rarely comes in, it is difficult to form a meaningful relationship.

For example, I witnessed the following interaction. A man entered the barbershop and climbed into the chair. The barber asked, "What will it be today?" The customer responded, "Same as last time." There was a pause, and then the barber said, "I don't remember ever cutting your hair." Quite offended, the customer exclaimed, "I got my last haircut in this very chair, by you! Not more than six months ago!" The barber retorted, "Well, if all my customers were that regular, I'd be on food stamps."

Women Hairstylists and the Unisex Shop

In the 1960s, young men who wanted their hair styled longer stopped going to traditional barbershops, because barbers could not—or would not—cut their hair properly. Some barbers were not trained in how to style long hair. Others refused to have long-haired men as customers for fear of offending other customers, or being viewed as supporting radical un-American ideas.

Wearing long hair, it was dangerous to go into a barbershop—or even walk by. When I was a youth and my hair was shoulder-length, I had barbers run out of their shops offering to cut my hair at no charge. I had others threaten to cut off my hair and another vital part of my anatomy as well.

When long-haired young men wanted to have their hair trimmed, they often went to women's beauty parlors where they found people used to cutting long hair. Over time, this trend contributed to the decline of the traditional barbershop. It was no longer hip to seen in a barbershop. Barbershops became seen as only for short-haired old men—even after longer hairstyles were incorporated into mainstream fashion and the political message was lost. As the young men who avoided barbershops in the 1960s became the fathers of the 1970s, '80s, and '90s, by habit they naturally took their sons to hairstylists instead of barbershops.

Since men were self-conscious to be seen in traditional women's beauty parlors, more unisex hairstyling salons opened. That way, a man could get his long hair cut and not have to sit next to an old lady with blue hair getting her nails done. The unisex shop even hit the White House. When Jimmy Carter was President, he replaced Milton Pitts—a barber who cut only men's hair—with a pair of unisex hairstylists. Mr. Pitts had cut hair in the White House basement during the Nixon and Ford administrations. When Reagan was elected President, he brought back Mr. Pitts on a part-time basis—perhaps the one thing Reagan did while in office that I actually liked.

Studies have shown that men with executive or managerial positions are more likely than other men to go to hairstylists rather than barbershops. Money and education are also factors. Of men making $60,000 or more per year, one in five use hairstylists, compared to only one in eight of men who bring in less than $20,000 per year (Tolstoi Wallach, 1987).

With so many men going to unisex shops or hairstylists,

a new generation of upper-middle-class boys have never stepped foot in a traditional barbershop. As grown men, will they be likely to reverse this trend? When I go into a barbershop and see, out in the open, the "boy board" (the padded board placed across a barber-chair's arms to elevate a boy to a height where the barber can comfortably cut his hair), I know I am in a shop with a future. Another generation of boys is being exposed to the culture of the barbershop. When I go into a shop and see no such board, I know that when the old customers die, the shop will close.

As human beings, we are neophobic. We are wary of new, unfamiliar situations and places. Since barbershops differ from hair salons in appearance and social atmosphere, they may seem strange and even frightening to someone who enters them for the first time. Middle class men who, as boys, had their hair cut only in salons would be nervous going into a barbershop where they did not know the social norms.

Barbershops used to be a place where the classes mingled, where banker, lawyer, and physician sat in the same chair as bricklayer, teamster, and miner. Now, haircutting establishments are more and more divided by class. This division has widespread social impact. Again, the concept of neophobia says that if members of different social classes are separated, they become less familiar and somewhat frightening to each other. The separation of classes leads easily to stereotyping, fear, and discrimination.

Rather than working together to solve common problems, too often we blame members of other social groups—whom we see and talk with less than in the days when neighborhood barbershops were places to sit and visit.

The Economic Advantages of Franchise Shops

Just as in the restaurant trade, the business of cutting hair is being taken over by franchised shops. In St. Paul, Minnesota, with a population of 272,000, when you look in the *Yellow Pages* under "Barbers" you will find 208 listings. However, 119 are also listed as "Beauty Salons;" 53 of these are franchised unisex hairstylists. That leaves only 89 listings that qualify as traditional barbershops. As with so many things in America, it comes down to money. The profits from a decently-managed franchise shop will be much greater than the best-run barbershop.

There are several reasons for this. First, most chain shops, such as *Cost Cutters* or *Great Expectations,* hire people with beauty-operator licenses. In most states, this requires less training than a barber's license. Individuals who get certified with less financial or time commitment are often willing to be paid a lower starting salary. Also, traditionally more women obtained beauty-operator licenses, and often were willing to work only part-time. The Bureau of Labor Statistics (1984) reported that in 1982, 39% of non-supervisory beauty-shop workers had part-time schedules. They averaged 29.6 hours per week. This generally means that owners pay less in employee benefits, keeping their overhead costs lower.

Furthermore, with larger staffs of part-time employees, franchise salons can and do stay open nights and Sundays.

Each chair can be used by several haircutters on different shifts. The only limit on the income then is the number of clients that can be attracted. In 1993, a franchised shop such as *Great Expectations* had an average gross of $300,000 per year. This is based on eight haircutters (each being paid $12,000 per year) who can give haircuts to a total of 375 customers per week, each customer paying at least $15 for the service.

Union barbershops, on the contrary, have a limited number of hours they can be open. The union prevents barbershops from staying open on Sundays or late in the evening. This was originally done to protect apprentices and new barbers from long hours. Prior to union agreements which specified opening and closing hours, nearby shops would compete with each other, opening a little earlier and closing a wee bit later to attract one or two more customers. This led to outrageous work hours. Before the formation of a union, the average journeyman-barber's work week stretched from 7:00 in the morning to 9:00 at night, Monday through Friday, plus 7:00 a.m. to midnight on Saturday—and Sunday morning as well so customers could get shaved prior to attending church services.

The average work week for a barber in 1927 was 72 hours per week. By 1931, conditions had improved only enough to decrease average hours to 70.8 per week. Unlike salons, most barbershops have only one or two workers, and the owner is usually one of these (Bureau of Labor Statistics, 1984).

Since many franchise-shop hairstylists are not owner/operators, but merely rent space in someone else's business, they are also more likely to move when the grass looks greener at another establishment. Therefore, it is harder for them to develop the same kind of history and commitment to one shop and its neighborhood that most barbers have.

In 1980, the Barber and Beauticians Union merged with the Food and Commercial Workers Union. Alone, the barbers and beauticians lacked the resources to organize workers in the franchise shops that are supplanting traditional independent shops. The Food and Commercial Workers Union was chosen because it represents many employees in the malls where many of the new haircutting franchises are located (Ruben, 1980).

Stagnant Prices

In 1983, you could obtain a haircut for a price that ranged from $4 to $120 (Kabatznick, 1983). Where could you find a $120 haircut, you ask? The answer is New York City, of course.

Barbers tend to charge half the fee that franchise hairsalons charge for a haircut. I talked with one barber who worked part-time in a regular barbershop and part-time in a hairstyling salon. He noted, "I do the same haircuts at both places, but the 'eight dollar' I do at the barbershop goes for twenty-nine bucks when I do it at the salon."

Young barbers have a difficult time raising the prices of their services. The greatest resistance often comes not from patrons but from fellow barbers. Barbers in the trade for years resist raising prices; they have already paid for their equipment or building, so their overhead is low. New barbers

To all our patrons,
For the past 14 years we have been fortunate enough to only raise our prices .50¢. However, due to the increase in expenses we have no other choice but to raise our price. Effective July 1, 1992 the price of a haircut will be $6.00.
Please note: Special hair artistry shall be priced accordingly.
Thank You
In the Guard and proud.
U.S.A.

can not charge higher prices if competing with well-established barbers. Especially if a barber's customers tend to be older men—many on fixed incomes—or men with lower-paying jobs, then that barber is likely to hear complaints if prices are increased. Older barbers have told me that the price of a haircut ought to be equal to the current legal minimum hourly wage.

Many barbers have a lower price for senior citizens. However, this is not always the case. I met one older barber (who did not tell me his age, but mentioned that his sister claims he is 78) who charged *more* than the usual price if the customer was 65 years or older. When I asked for the rationale, he replied, "Those guys figure since they are old they can get by being crabby and too damn fussy. I don't need the aggravation. I hope the price keeps them away."

One author (Phillips, 1995) postulated that male ego has something to do with why barbers have trouble raising their prices. He believes that, unlike women who secretly take pride in spending large amounts on their hair and appearance, men take pride in exactly the opposite. They are proud of how little they spend on their appearance—and that includes their haircare.

I have noticed that some customers think that they ought to pay by how much hair is removed, as if it takes less skill or time to cut off a half-inch of hair compared to a full inch. I liked the way one barber handled a customer. The man walked into the shop and asked, "How much is it for a haircut?" "Seven and a half," replied the barber. As the customer began to sit in the barber's chair, he asked, "How much for just a trim?" The barber responded, "If your butt touches my chair, the fee is seven-fifty ... regardless of how much hair you have or don't have when you stand up again."

In 1947, the standard price for a haircut was 75¢—the equivalent of about $5 today—and a shave was going for 35¢—about $2.40 today (J.B.H.C., 1947). In the 1930s, during the Great Depression, some barbers managed to stay in business by bartering for their services.

> Barbers Swap Haircuts for Sparta Wheat.
> Sparta, Michigan. Oct. 16 (AP). The barbers of Sparta have agreed to cut hair for wheat. For one bushel of wheat any farmer living in these parts can obtain an artistic hair cut and 27 cents cash farm relief.
> The decision to accept wheat instead of money was reached at a meeting of all Sparta tonsorial artists at which the present plight of the agricultural industry was discussed. Wheat is selling here for 67 cents a bushel and a trim is valued at 40 cents. Chickens belonging to Sparta barbers will profit by the offer. [*St. Paul Dispatch*, in *Krank's Review*, November 1930]

One rule of barbershop etiquette I learned the hard way. Do not ask, "How many haircuts do you do a day?" You will likely get the answer, "All of them. I'm the only barber here, aren't I?" I must have asked this question hundreds of times without ever getting a straight answer. I was so dense that one barber finally made it clear that my question was out of line when he responded, "Look, I didn't ask you how much

you make. Don't ask me what I make."

Until recently, barbers often owned their own small buildings. Today, however, since prices have stagnated, new barbers often do not generate enough income to afford to buy their own shop; they rent space from a landlord. If the landlord raises the rent, the barber is hard-pressed to pass the cost on to his customers as most businesses do.

I could always tell a well-established barber from a new barber by the way they behaved as I approached a shop to photograph it. Old barbers merely watched me as I walked towards the door. New barbers would stop what they were doing, and rush out to ask me what I was up to. They had seen my camera, and were afraid that I was a realtor, photographing the building to place an ad to sell it. The elderly barbers owned their small buildings, and were not afraid that their livelihood was about to be sold out from under them.

If a barber does not own the building where his shop is located, and cannot afford rent increases, he might be forced to relocate the shop to a less expensive part of the building, like a basement or second-floor locale. Such a move has severe impact on business. Long-time customers are willing to walk up or down one floor, but without the benefit of a street-level window with a barber pole in it, potential new customers do not as easily know there is even a shop in the building.

A sign of a quality hotel used to be a full-service barbershop on the main floor, right off the lobby. But nowadays, if there is a shop, it often has been relocated to some obscure corner of the building, thereby losing many impulse customers. The space the barbershop once proudly occupied is now likely turned into a gift shop. Souvenir objects, t-shirts, and postcards have become more important than a relaxing shoe shine, a trim, and some friendly conversation.

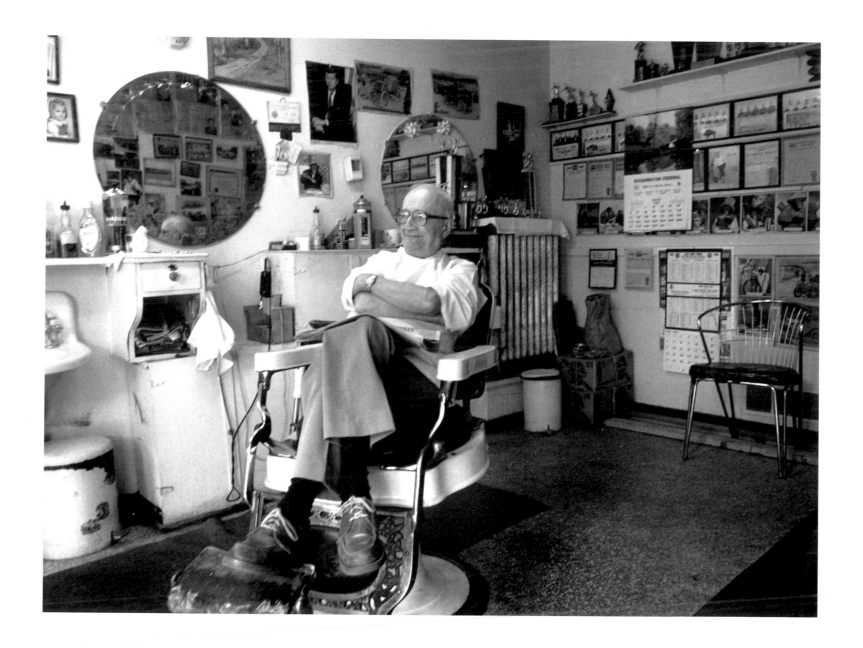

CHAPTER TWELVE

The Future of Barbershops

Long hours, miserable compensation, cheap, unfair competitive prices [in America in the 1800s] continued to maintain barbering as a secondary occupation.

—*Journeymen Barbers, Hairdressers, and Cosmetologists International Union of America,* Practical and Scientific Barbering *(1934)*

Although these words were written to describe the state of American barbering in the 1800s, some barbers would argue that they accurately describe current conditions. Barbering is an occupation to avoid if you have expensive tastes. One barber, trying to look for the silver lining, told me, "I don't worry about not making much money. I have to work such long hours that I don't have time to spend the money I do bring in."

The situation is so bleak that most of the barbers I talked with, even those with several generations of barbering in their family, did not want their son (or daughter) to become a barber. One barbershop had been run by four generations of the same family, but was about to close permanently because nobody in the next generation was interested in taking it over. Another shop had been in continuous existence since the 1700s, but was destined to close in two months for lack of a new barber to replace the man who was retiring.

Even shops so busy that the barbers are overworked have

trouble finding a barber to hire. Grey's Barber Shop in Hayward, Wisconsin, where the motto is: "$8.50 and 10 minutes is all it takes to leave looking sleek," ran the following ad for eight months in four daily and 234 weekly newspapers, and did not receive a single response:

"Wanted: Real man to cut real men's hair at real barbershop in northern Wisconsin. Must be able to talk hunting and fishing with customers. Only barbershop in town. Virtually no competitors for 100 miles. Weekends off to scout for deer. Sissies need not apply." [Maller, 1995]

For all I know, they are still a barber short. If you are a real barber—and a real man—maybe you could get hired.

A wave of new barbers entered the field after World War II, many attending school with the help of the G.I. Bill. Now, fifty years later, most barbers of that generation have reached the age of retirement, leaving barbershops across the country searching for replacements (Phillips, 1995).

When I asked one barber if any of his children were planning to follow in his footsteps, taking over the shop when he retired, he practically screamed, "Not if I have anything to say about it! I told them to get a job that has paid vacations and a decent retirement plan. I'll be working beside this chair till I drop. I paid for all six of my kids' education—one haircut at a time—but only after they made a promise to me that they would go to college and not become barbers."

I found many barbers had another sideline to supplement their income. I met barbers who prepared taxes, sold real estate, fixed small engines, sold knives or bait. Doug Shaffer of Goshen, Indiana, not only cuts hair in his shop, he also sells sports memorabilia. He has old mitts, posters, trading cards, and pennants for sale. His chair sits at the home plate of a miniature baseball diamond, complete with bases and a rubber for the pitcher's mound. His customers wait their turn in a dugout.

Despite how poorly barbering pays, nearly every barber I talked with said he enjoyed his job. As one told me, "Being a barber means that every 15 minutes you have successfully completed a job. What other job gives you that satisfaction? I've been to a lot of barber meetings in my day. I have yet to hear a single barber say that he dreads to open up in the morning."

I once overheard a customer ask one of the barbers, "You still in school working on that master's degree in math?" The barber just kept on clipping and replied, "I finished that degree last semester. Now I'm working on my Ph.D." After a moment the customer responded, "Well, I supposed you'll close up shop when you finish that one, hey?" The barber smiled as he said, "Nope. But you can bet I'll be raising my prices."

I was impressed with how fun-loving the vast majority of the barbers were. Usually I could hear the laughter pouring out as I approached the door. I do not know if people attracted to barbering are easy-going from the start or if the barbershop environment has this effect on them. One afternoon, a customer made a similar observation when he noted aloud to the barber and the others sitting about, "Say, we all

graduated from high school the same year, didn't we? And look at us. We all have gray hair or are bald. 'Cept you. You have a head full of black hair. How does that figure?" The barber's response was immediate. "I'm the only barber in the bunch. Barbers don't have any worries."

In all the years I have wandered into barbershops throughout the country, meeting hundreds of barbers, I have only been treated disrespectfully by one man. "How's business today?" I asked cheerfully. "None of your goddamn business," he snorted, glaring at me from across the room. I tried again. "My hobby is making photographs of barbershops, and I wonder if you would mind if I included yours in my collection?" I asked somewhat less cheerfully. "I don't give a damn if you include my shop in your collection or not," he barked, getting out of the chair and waving his arms about his head. "I assume that's your version of, 'No, I'd rather you didn't take any photographs of my shop,'" I replied. "You can just get out right now, and don't ever come back either. I'm trying to make a buck here. I don't have time for your kind," he yelled as I made a hasty exit. I was more surprised than angry. I figured I had just caught him at a bad time; after all, he had been cutting hair in that same shop for over fifty years—and was wearing a neck brace.

Although I met only one truly grumpy barber in all my years, a few tried to convince me otherwise. One day, as I drove down the main street of a small midwestern town, I stopped at the first barbershop I spotted and inquired of the barber within, "How many barbershops in town?" "Four shops and five barbers," he responded in a friendly tone of voice. When I explained my mission, he agreed to be photographed, but added, "I'm sure most of the other fellows will be happy to help you out, but there is one guy that is cranky. He won't cooperate. But don't take it personal. He's like that with everybody. The whole town has gotten used to it."

After photographing that shop, I wandered down the street to the next shop, poked my head in the doorway, and announced, "I hear there are five barbers in town, and one of you is grumpy." "I've been called worse," chuckled the barber. After completing my photographs there, I strode to the third shop and repeated the rumor of the grumpy barber in town. "I bet it was that S.O.B. on the corner that told you that, and I'll bet he said it was me!" laughed the third barber. I made my way to the fourth shop. As I plopped down in a chair, I again said I had been informed there was a cranky barber to be found in town. "That would be my partner over there behind the next chair," grinned the fourth barber, pointing to the man beside him. "Me? I always heard it was you that was the cranky one!" laughed the fifth barber. I never did determine which of the five men was the cranky barber.

When I talked with barbers about the decline of the traditional shop, most of them expressed sadness rather than anger. They might mention that the dwindling of shops is due to long hair or some other factor, but usually without a tone of bitterness or blame, only sadness.

I often asked the barbers I visited what they thought the future would bring to the world of barbering. One man predicted, "Computerized haircuts. You'll put your head in a

machine and it will do the work. And people will be in such a hurry, they'll want drive-in barbershops. They will just drive up and stick their head out the window into a machine."

Perhaps barbershops will return to their itinerant roots. In the 10th century, street barbers wore belts with hooks for their tools, and gave haircuts on the side of the road. In the 1930s and '40s, barbers used to make house calls to hospitals and house-bound customers. That sounds similar to what one Colorado barber, a woman, is doing today. She started a company to provide haircuts to people in their offices. She had to get a variance from the Board of Barbers and Cosmetologists, and the Health Board had to approve her procedures and portable equipment (Brokaw, 1988). But she convinced them and is busy snipping away. This type of service may be a time-saver for the customer, but I cannot help but think it sounds boring. I spend enough time in my office without getting my hair cut there as well. Going to a barbershop used to be a social event.

Who knows? The future of the barbershop may be found at *The Mane Event*, a men's hair-salon where women stylists cut your hair—while modeling the latest lingerie. In addition to seeing the stylist working on his head, a customer can see the other stylists in the salon's wall-to-wall mirrors. Customers are screened through a glass partition, and there is a security button connected directly to the local police station. In addition to the usual hair-care services and products, customers can purchase lingerie (Breisch, 1992).

Then again, maybe the future of the traditional barber-shop lies with the richness of its culture. The heart of the barbershop's appeal is the man-to-man interaction that can be found there. We can only hope our society will realize the importance of such gathering places, sparking a renewal of interest in the traditional barbershop as one of Oldenburg's "Third Places"—a comfortable, congenial renaissance of the pleasures of just being a guy.

A similar renaissance has occurred in another field of interest to men: beer-making. In the not-so-distant past, numerous local breweries existed that produced excellent regional beers. Over the years, these small factories were bought out by large corporations that all but eliminated the regional labels to mass-produce beers designed to appeal to consumers from across America. The American beers became more and more similar until they were nearly identical. The image of the brand, the manner it was advertised, and price became the chief factors that determined which beer most drinkers bought.

However, a few years ago, small breweries once again began to appear. Now called micro-breweries, these local operations could honestly brag that "we produce less beer in a month than the major producers spill in a day." The small breweries found many men willing to spend a little more money to drink a quality product. The diverse taste and improved freshness of regional beers proved important to those consumers who stopped to think about what they really wanted to drink.

Hopefully, just as local beers have made a comeback, so too will we see a revival of the traditional American barbershop and all it has to offer us. Next time you order a locally-made beer, drink a toast to the health and happiness of your neighborhood barber—and barbers everywhere.

And the next time you need a haircut ... well, you should know by now where to go.

CHAPTER THIRTEEN

The Last Day

I had already spent most of the morning and afternoon photographing several other shops, but since I was only going to be in this town one more day, I hoped to get another shop done before day's end. As I pulled up, the barber was just locking the door.

"Will you be open tomorrow?" I asked in disappointment. "Nope. Not tomorrow, or the next day, or even the day after that. Not never again," he replied quietly through the narrow opening of the doorway. "I figure after 65 years on my feet, I deserve to sit down for the rest of my life and take it easy."

I pled my case, insisting that he had an obligation to barbering to let me in to photograph him on his final day. The lock clicked open and the door swung wide. "After over six decades, I guess I can spare a few extra minutes," he muttered as he shuffled back into the shop.

The minutes turned to hours. The hours filled to the brim with stories. How as a young barber, fresh out of barber school, he had overheard a customer talking about where the trolley car tracks were going to be laid. How he took his lunch break that same day, took his savings out of the bank, and bought a tiny plot of land right on the future trolley-line. How he and his buddies constructed the shop in the evenings after their regular jobs—as the city crews were laying the tracks. How his shop opened on the same day—not by coincidence—as the ceremonies held to celebrate the initial run of the city's new trolley system. How for years after, "the working man's automobile" stopped right in front of his shop, so the guys could get a shave and trim before going home after work. How it helped the men unwind before they got home to their wives and kids—a chance to shake a few hands, slap some backs, tell a joke, crack a smile.

That was until Henry Ford and the "Big Three" automakers saw to it that every man drove to work by himself in his own car. Then the highway came in, and foot traffic dried up. Still the barber made a living, but the bustle was gone.

"So what? There is something to be said for a relaxing, slower pace. A man can't stand too many years of a shop full of laughing noisy men, all waiting their turn. Gets on the nerves, having to give a good cut but always mindful of how many are waiting. Couldn't have kept up that pace for all these years. Worked out better this way," he observed.

"What will happen to the shop now that you're retiring?" I wondered aloud.

"Sold the land," he said, as if that explained everything.

"The land? What about the shop itself?" I asked.

"Too small to be of any use. They're gonna bulldoze it," he answered, trying to sound as if he did not care.

"I suppose you sold another barber all your equipment, the chair ... " I guessed.

"Nope. Couldn't find an old barber that didn't already have what he needed. Young ones don't want the old-fashioned stuff. It's all going to the guy that bought the land. Package deal. Saves me the trouble of having to haul it to the dump," his voice trailing off.

We sat in silence as the sun went down, the tiny shop getting dark. Finally he got up, went to the back of the room, and returned with a barber pole.

"Marvy 55?" I guessed.

"Boy, you have spent a lot of time in barbershops," he marveled. Pointing to the pole, he noted, "They broke the glass, some kids probably. I never fixed it. Too expensive. You want it? I can't use it. I'd give you the rest of the stuff if I could. But like I said—'package deal.'"

"I understand," I said, as I took the pole from him.

"You sure you're not a barber?" he asked hopefully.

"I'm positive," I responded.

"Your dad?" he wondered.

"No, he's a psychologist, too," I said, hoping I was not disappointing him too much.

"Grandfather?" he kept trying.

"Not him either," I responded, knowing this time that I was disappointing him.

After a while he continued, "You missed your calling."

"Maybe," I nodded.

"It's not too late. You're still young. How old are you?" he asked with renewed cheer in his voice.

"Thirty," I said, knowing I was receiving a compliment from this old man.

"Hell, you're still a pup. Look at me, been cutting hair since I was twenty—and I'm 85 years young," he said, sitting up straight in his chair. "Ever thought of going to barber college?" he said, leaning towards me.

"Not seriously," I confessed.

"Too bad. You'd have made a fine barber. You understand people," he pronounced as he laid his wrinkled hand on my shoulder.

After a few seconds, I did not know what else to say, so I settled for, "Well ... I appreciate your hospitality and cooperation. It's late."

"Yes. It is late," he agreed. He walked me to the door, unlocked it, and let me out. "I locked the door out of habit," he explained. "If a customer gets through the door, you've got to cut his hair—no matter how long after closing it is, or how many cuts you've already done that day. It's an unwritten rule."

"I can see where that would be a problem," I said, nodding.

He slowly shut the door behind me, and locked it once again. From my car I could see him shuffle over to his old chair and slump down, resting his head in his wrinkled hands. "What is he thinking?" I wondered. His last day after all these years. Did he know he was doing his last haircut when he did it? Or did he think at the time there would be just one more? If he did realize that he was doing his last work as a barber, I bet it was one hell of a haircut.

Sixty-five years, standing in the same four-foot circle, around the same chair. No cake. No party. No gold watch. I wish now I had gone back and asked for the honor of being his final customer. And then I would offer to buy him dinner. I regret not doing it to this day.

A Questionnaire

If you have read the part of this book that tells about me, you already know that I usually write self-help books. One of the habits I have developed as a result is that I am constantly trying to figure out how to help you, the reader, personalize and apply the material I am writing about to your life. I thought this book would be my first that would not attempt this feat.

I was wrong. In doing my literature search, I stumbled across James H. McAlexander and John W. Schouten's (1989) research on "Hair Style Changes As Transition Markers," which they did at Iowa State University. They gave 84 college juniors and seniors a questionnaire on "consumer behavior." A portion of this research included a list of excellent questions which they asked their subjects—and which I will now pass on to you.

"Now & in the past, what has been important to you in your selection of hairstyles?"

"What has been important in your selection of hair providers?" (I think they mean hair*care* providers. I think only God can make a hair.)

"How would you describe your current hairstyle?"

"What other kinds of hairstyles have you worn prior to this?"

"Why have there been major changes?"

"When did they occur?"

"What brought them about?"

"What does your hair communicate about you?"

"Who cuts your hair?"

"How did you select this person?"

"What was important to you in making this selection?"

"How often have you changed hair care providers?"

"Why?" (This is the world's shortest research question—short and to the point!)

"How much do you pay for haircuts?"

"How often do you get your hair cut and/or styled?"

"Do you ever cut your own hair?"

"Why?"

And finally, one question of my own:

What did you learn about yourself from responding to these questions?

The Barbering Hall of Fame

Every professional group has a way to honor those who make outstanding contributions to their field. In entertainment, there are Emmies, Grammies, and Oscars. For barbers, the pinnacle is being selected to the Barbering Hall of Fame. This illustrious pantheon can be found at the site of the Barber Museum and Library in Canal Winchester, a suburb of Columbus, Ohio. The following is a partial list (by year of induction) of those who have been honored, with some of the accomplishments which earned them a place in barbering history.

1965. A. B. Moler started the first barber school in America, in Chicago in 1893. He also wrote seven books on barbering.

1966. L. Sherman Trusty published barbering text books, and founded four barber schools in California.

1968. Louis E. McIlvain was elected General Organizer for the Master Barber/Beauty Association in 1924. In 1929, he was elected General Secretary, a post he held until he retired in 1953.

1968. Charles De Zemler became an American citizen in 1921 after immigrating from Sweden. He owned three barbershops in Rockefeller Center in New York City, which at their peak employed 58 barbers, and authored *Once Over Lightly*, a history of barbering.

1970. William Birthright was a long-serving General President of the Barbers' International Union.

1970. Matthew Andis spent fifty years designing and manufacturing professional barber clippers. He was responsible for the electric magnetic clippers that replaced hand and cable-drive clippers. Andis Clippers are still used in barbershops.

1972. George Bynum, from Illinois, was the only barber to be elected Vice-President of the Illinois State Federation of Labor.

1972. Raymond E. Andrew was the founder of the Barber Hall of Fame (that's one way to get in, I suppose) and the Library for the Hair Industry. He was also President of the Ohio Barber Schools Association and the National Associa-

tion of Barber Schools. He wrote *The Teachers' Manual of the Andrew Method of Barbering* and *The Director's Manual of the Andrew Method of Barbering*.

1972. John Oster invented the Oster motor-driven hand-clipper (1924), the Stim-U-Lax massage machine (1935), and the Oster Lather machine (1937).

1973. Frank Marchese was President of the National Association of Barber Boards and Secretary of the Barbers' Local #341 of Patterson, New Jersey, and for fourteen years, Secretary of the National Association of Barber Boards.

1973. Buck Ashmore served on the Florida Barbers Board for six years, then became President of the National Association of Barber Boards of America.

1975. Edmond Roffler was the developer of the Roffler Sculptur-Kut [sic] techniques, a method in which over 6,000 barbers have been trained.

1976. Nick Cimaglia was the author of numerous barbering books still used as textbooks in barber schools. His works include: *The Tonsorial Artist* (1924)—"tonsorial" means pertaining to clipping, *The Theory and Practice of Barbering* (1932), *The National Barber School Journal* (1950), *Men's Hairstyling as Your Career* (1965), and the film *For the Love of Your Hair* (1975).

1982. William Marvy started his barber supply business in 1936 and saw it grow to become the largest of its kind in the Midwest. In 1950, he began manufacturing a type of barber pole that became a classic. He sold over 70,000 poles in his lifetime. It is likely that most of the barber poles you have seen were made in St. Paul, Minnesota, by Mr. Marvy's

employees.

1988. Robert Blake Powell was a freelance writer for *Professional Men's Hairstylist*. He also wrote *Antique Shaving Mugs of the United States* (the mug-collectors "bible"), *Occupational and Fraternal Shaving Mugs in the United States*, and *Great American Barber Chairs and Barberiana Collectibles*.

1989. Richard A. Plumb was editor for *The Journeyman Barber and Beauty Culture* for ten years. He served as Vice President/Director of the Barbers, Cosmetologist Division of the United Food and Commercial Workers International and was President of the Barbers, Beauticians and Allied Industries International. He also authored *Ancient and Honorable Barber Profession* and *The Monthly Plumb Line*.

1989. Kenneth F. Stone was the Director of the Andrew Barber College in Columbus, Ohio, for fourteen years. He served as President of both the Ohio Barber Schools Association (nine years) and the National Association of Barber Schools, and edited *The N.A.B.S. Newsletter*. At one time in his life, he owned four private barber schools.

1990. Jacob Yahm acted as Head of Examinations for the State of New York for thirty years. He authored the New York State Barber Board's examination Review Book and created a system of testing for barbering which is used in many states today. He co-authored *The Standard Textbook of Professional Barber/Styling*, and contributed to *The National Beauty School Journal* and *The National-Interstate Council Bulletin*.

1990. James Don Knauss was first licensed as a barber in 1966. A barber investigator for a dozen years, he was then the director of the California Barber Board for 26 years and was

twice President of the National Association of Barber Boards. He authored a training manual for barber apprentices, and wrote for *Journeyman Barber* and *Master Barber Magazine*.

1991. Dennis Roth became licensed as a barber in 1934. He authored two books of jokes commonly told in barbershops. He currently demonstrates the art of shaving to thousands of visitors each year at the Sauder Museum in Archbold, Ohio.

1991. Elijah Pierce was born in 1892 in Baldwyn, Mississippi, the son of an ex-slave. In 1921, he became a barber in Ohio, a trade he practiced for the next 52 years. He also became famous as a woodcarver, his visionary work rising to prominence in major American art galleries and museums. He was awarded a National Heritage Fellowship from the National Endowment for the Arts in 1982 for his carving. He died in 1984.

1992. Edwin C. Jeffers is the owner and curator of the largest library on hair and the largest barber museum in the world. It measures 4,000 square feet and contains material dating back to the 1700s. He was licensed as a barber in 1957 and rose to become Executive Director of the Ohio Barber Board, Executive Officer of the National Association of Barber Boards, and National Director of Examinations.

If you know of any barbers you think ought to be a part of the Barbering Hall of Fame, you could write Ed Jeffers at the Barber Museum, 2 South High Street, Canal Winchester, Ohio 43110, or arrange a visit to the museum near Columbus (open by appointment). The displays feature six barbershops from different eras beginning in the 1790s, as well as over 500 shaving mugs, 600 razors, and 50 types of barber poles.

As impressive as the Hall of Fame is, there are some persons conspicuous by their absence, even to a non-barber like myself. For example, I would nominate: Richard le Barbour, the first Master Barber and Supervisor of the Trade in London in 1308; Mr. Middleditch, the last practicing barber-surgeon, who died in 1826; and Edward Finkelstone, elected first President of the Journeymen Barbers' International Union of America on December 5, 1887.

I would also include Joe Cirello. Joe, who started out as a Philadelphia barber, is credited with creating the "D.A.," or "Duck's Ass," hairstyle. Although the D.A. is usually thought of as a hairstyle of the 1950s, he started cutting his customers' hair in this style in 1938. At that time, he called it the "Swing Cut." He used it to enter a hairstyling contest in New York City. He won, and was awarded a ten-year contract cutting hair at Warner Brothers' Hollywood studios.

Mr. Cirello can claim the honor of "lowering the ears" of Sinatra, Bogart, Elvis, Bill Haley, John Travolta, Henry Winkler, Michael Caine, Wayne Newton, and Boy George. He even gave James Dean his last haircut before he rode off to his demise (Geist, 1986).

Henny Youngman, "The King of the One-liners," once told me he knew a barber who had owned 200 barbershops. That must be some kind of a record. If a barber like that does not belong in the Hall of Fame, at least he ought to be listed

in the *Guinness Book of World Records.*

By the way, when I talked with Mr. Youngman, he told me he used to get his hair cut at a shop where "two Italian guys would show up with guitars and play while the barber cut. You know, those Italian songs. La, la, la, la, la. Of course, they wanted a tip. Which they got. Sometimes."

I neglected to ask Mr. Youngman what he says to his barber when he sits down for a trim. I hope he says, "Take my hair—please!"

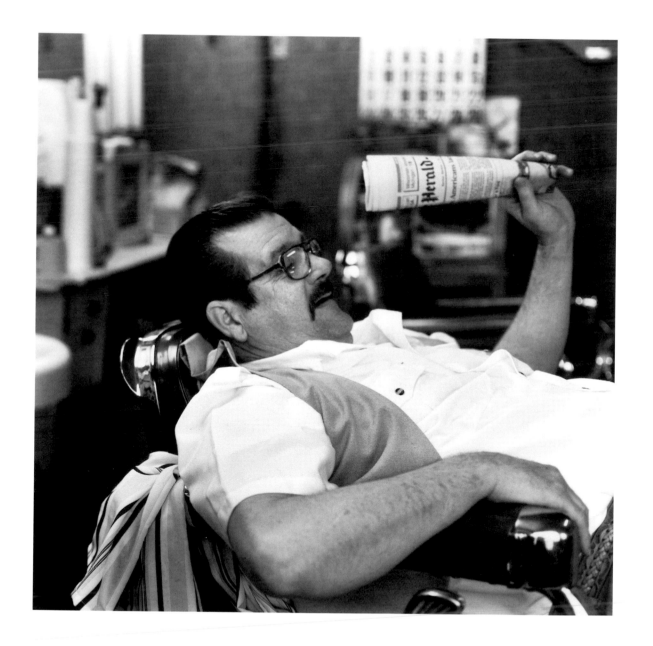

168

APPENDIX C

References and Additional Readings

Andrews, William. (1904). *At the Sign of the Barber Pole*. Cottingham, Yorkshire: J.R. Tutin. Reissued by Singing Tree Press, Detroit, 1969.

Associated Master Barbers of America. (1931). *Standardized Textbook of Barbering*. Chicago.

Beaver, David. (1984). "Barbering," *The Fiddlehead* (No. 139, p. 23). Fredericton, New Brunswick, Canada: Depts. of English, University of New Brunswick and St. Thomas University.

Bauer, Fred. (1991). "The barber's son," *Reader's Digest* (March, p. 55–59).

Behar, R. (1986). "The cutter gets clipped," *Forbes* (March 24, p. 84–86).

Berg, Charles (1951). *The Unconscious Significance of Hair*. London.

Blount, Roy. (1986). *It Grows on You: A Hair-raising Survey of Human Plumage*. Garden City, New York: Doubleday and Co.

Brand, Horst and Ahmed, Ziaul Z. (1986). "Beauty and barber shops: the trend of labor productivity," *Monthly Labor Review* (109:21–26, March).

Breisch, Sandra Lee. (1992). "For some customers of this shop, the longer the wait, the better." *The Wall Street Journal* (June 19).

Brokaw, L. (1988). "Hair today, gone ... oh, forget it," *Inc.* (March, p. 18).

Bureau of Labor Statistics. (1984). *Occupational Projections and Training Data* (Bulletin 2206).

Clark, T. (1988). *From the Barber's Chair*. Minneapolis: Nodin Press.

Cooper, Bernard. (1990). "Nick's Barber Shop," *Harper's Magazine* (June, p. 38).

Cooper, Wendy. (1971). *Hair: Sex, Society, Symbolism*. London: Aldus Books; also New York: Stein and Day.

Cosby, Bill. (No date given). *Bill Cosby is a Very Funny Fellow. Right!* Warner Brother Records #1518.

De Zemler, Charles. (1939). *Once Over Lightly: The Story of Man and His Hair*. New York: Author. (Contains a bibliography of obscure and foreign-language references on barbering.)

Downs, E. (No date given). "The ultimate barber pole maker," *Northliner Magazine*.

Duhe, C. (1988). "A cut above: sitting in the barber's chair need not present a gamble," *Esquire* (March, p. 163).

Dyer, Isadore. (1905). "The barber shop in society," *New Orleans Medical and Surgical Journal* (August reprint).

Emerson, Ralph Waldo. (1968). *Essays and Journals*. New York: Doubleday and Co.

Exter, Thomas. (1990). "Beauty parlor and the beast," *American Demographics* (12:6, November).

Feinsilber, Mike and Mead, William B. (1980). *American Averages: Amazing Facts of Everyday Life*. Garden City, New York. Dolphin Books.

Firth, Raymond. (1973). *Symbols: Public and Private*. London: Allen and Unwin.

Flick, David. (1995). "Still making the cut: barber, 91, keeps trimming, talking away in small town," *The Dallas Morning News* (June 14, pp. 1 and 7).

Franklin, Clyde W. II. (1985). "Black male urban barbershops as sex role socialization," *Sex Roles* (12:965–979, May).

Fridman, Eric. (1991). "Haircut (barbering in America is becoming a forgotten art)," *American Scholar* (60.3:433–439, Summer).

Gales, P. (1992). From an August 18th letter to the author from the Norelco Consumer Products Company, Stamford, Ct.

Geist, William. (1986). "Mr. D.A.," *Esquire* (June, p. 288–291).

Giovannini, Joseph. (1987). "A matter of style," *The New York Times Magazine* (October 18, p. 54).

Givens, R. (1985). "Hair: a mecca for the hip," *Newsweek* (August 12, p. 12).

Graeber, L. (1990). "Saving face: the daily drudgery of shaving does not have to include pain," *New York Times Magazine* (Sept. 16, p. 34).

Hallpike, C.R. (1969). "Social hair," *Man* (9:256–64).

Hirsev, G. (1987). "Twenty years of rock & roll style," *Rolling Stone* (April 23, p. 97).

Hix, Charles. (1981). *Looking Good: A Guide for Men*. New York: Hawthorne Books.

Hutton, W. (1968). *Primitive Secret Societies*. New York: Octagon.

Jones, Norman. (1983). "Barbershop blues," *New Statesman* (106:12–13, July 22).

Jones, D. (1990). *Haircults: Fifty Years of Styles and Cuts*. London: Thames and Hudson.

Journeymen Barbers, Hairdressers, and Cosmetologists International Union of America. (1934). *Practical and Scientific Barbering*. Indianapolis, Indiana. (No longer in print).

Kabatznick, Ronna M. (1983). "Haircut phobias," *Psychology Today* (17:24–25, February).

Kernan, M. & Selig, J. (1991). "Short on the top, clippers on the sides and taper the back," *Smithsonian* (2.2:110–115, May).

Klobuchar, Jim. (1988). "The hands of Father Time clip right along," *Star Tribune* (June 29, p. 1B). Minneapolis, Minnesota.

Krank (19?–19?), *Krank's Review*. (No longer in print).

Krumholz, Phillip. (1989). "The barber pole: symbol with a past and a future," *Antiques and Collecting* (94.1, March, p. 69).

Krumholz, Phillip. (1992). *A History of Shaving and Razors*. Bartonville, Illinois: Ad Libs Publishing Co.

Leach, E.A. (1958). "Magical hair," *Journal of the Royal Anthropological Institute* (Vol. 88: 147–64, July–Dec., Part II).

Least Heat Moon, William. (1982). *Blue Highways*. Boston: Houghton Mifflin Co.

Legler, Gretchen. (1985). "Stripes forever," *Twin Cities* (January, p. 44–45).

Lidz, Franz. (1990). "From hair to eternity," *Sports Illustrated* (73.24:88–103).

MacDougal, M.J., Jr. (1967). *The Modern Barber*. New York: Exposition Press.

Maller, Peter. (1995). "Wanted: barber who can cut it," *Milwaukee Journal Sentinel* (April 28).

Margolies, John. (1984). "The last barber pole factory," *Gentlemen's Quarterly* (December, pp. 254 and 293).

McAlexander, James H. and Schouten, John W. (1989). "Hair style changes as transition markers," *Sociology and Social Research* (74:58–62, October).

McFalan, D., Editor. (1992). *The Guinness Book of Records*. New York: Facts on File.

Mead, Margaret. (1949). "Ways of the Body," chapter in *Male and Female*. New York: Morrow Quill.

Molloy, John T. (1976). *Dress for Success*. New York: Warner Books.

Moreau, D. and Kainen, B. (1990). "How to buy a haircut," *Changing Times* (May, p. 75).

Morris, Desmond. (1967). *The Naked Ape*. New York: McGraw-Hill.

Murphy, Austin. (1990). "Have sports gone to his head? An Indiana barber gives customers more than haircuts," *Sports Illustrated* (June 18, p. 8–10).

Murphy, H. L. (1990). "Wahl keeps clipping along with fashion-conscious line," *Crain's Chicago Business* (March 5, p. 4).

National Association of Barber Schools. (1972). "Barber school, barber students & barber statistics," *Research Report No. 6A* (revised July 1). Lincoln, Nebraska.

——. (1990). "Barber school, barber students & barber statistics," *Research Report No. 6A* (revised April 1). Lincoln, Nebraska.

Oldenburg, Ray. (1989). *The Great Good Place: Cafes, Coffee Shops, Community Centers, Beauty Parlors, General Stores, Bars, Hangouts, and How They Get You Through the Day*. New York: Paragon House.

Oxford University Press. (1970). *The New English Bible*. Oxford.

Phillips, Stephen. (1995). "Shortage of barbers has some working at fast clip," *Star Tribune* (May 15), Minneapolis, Minnesota. Orig. published in *Cleveland Plain Dealer*.

Reisner, J. (1985). "Koken Manufacturing Company: life on the cutting edge," *St. Louis Business Journal* (August 12, p. 48–51).

Robinson, Dwight E. (1976). "Fashions in shaving and trimming the beard: the men of the Illustrated London News, 1842–1972," *American Journal of Sociology* (81.5: 1133–9).

Rose, C. (1990). "Rolling with the wet set: cult of the haircut," *New Statesman and Society* (May 11, p. 46).

Ruben, G. (1980). "Barbers and Beauticians Union plans merger," *Monthly Labor Review* (March, p. 57–56).

Ryder, M. (1973). *Hair (Studies in Biology No. 41)*. London: Edward Arnold.

Rylant, Cynthia. (1994). In Evans, Walker (photographs) and Rylant, Cynthia (poetry). *Something Permanent*. New York: Harcourt Brace & Company.

Sadick, Neil S. (1991). *Your Hair: Helping to Keep It (Treatment and Prevention of Hair Loss for Men and Women)*. Yonkers, New York: Consumer Reports Books.

Simmel, Georg. (1971). *Georg Simmel On Individuality and Social Forms*. Chicago: The University of Chicago Press.

Slater, Philip E. (1971). "Must marriage cheat today's young women?" *Redbook Magazine* (February). Quoted in *The Great Good Place*, by Ray Oldenburg.

Synnott, Anthony. (1987). "Shame and glory: a sociology of hair," *British Journal of Sociology* (38:381–413 S).

Thorpe, S. (1951). *Practice and Science of Standard Barbering*. New York: Milady Publishing.

Tolstoi Wallach, A. (1987). "Hairpower: haircuts for male executives," *The New York Times Magazine* (Sept. 20, p. 70).

Trusty, L. Sherman. (1960). *The Art and Science of Barbering*. Los Angeles: Wolfen.

United States Bureau of the Census. (1991). *Statistical Abstract of the United States* (111th ed.). Washington, D.C.

United States Department of Commerce. (1923). *Fourteenth Census of the United States* (Vol. IV). Washington, D.C.

———. (1933). *Fifteenth Census of the United States: 1930* (Vol. V). Washington, D.C.

———. (1976). *Historical Statistics of the United States*. Washington, D.C.

Wallis, Claudia. (1983). "Stress: can we cope?" *Time* (June 6).

Warner Brothers. (1991). "The Bunny of Seville," in *Bugs Bunny's Overtures to Disaster* (video tape).

Wasserman, Norman. (1988). "The seven-month itch (barbers and girlfriends)," *The New York Times Magazine* (March 13, p. 54).

Weisman, John. (1988). "The barbershop," *Gentlemen's Quarterly* (58.10:225–228, October).

Wilderson, Frank B. III. (1989). *Incognegro: The Prism of an Honorary Whiteman* (unpublished manuscript).

175

About the Author

Mic Hunter is an amateur documentary photographer whose main claim to fame to date has come through sales of one single photograph to a number of magazines in the U.S. and Europe. This image of hundreds of ladybugs massed together in a blaze of red, black, and white has appeared in the magazines *Omni*, *Stern*, *Oggi Natura*, and *Bunte*. The Hazelden Foundation released it as a poster to be used in substance-abuse treatment programs.

Mr. Hunter makes his living as a psychotherapist. He has traveled widely to give talks across the country, and has appeared on major television talk shows. He is the author of *Abuse Boys: The Neglected Victims of Sexual Abuse*; *The Twelve Steps and Shame*; and *Recovering From Shame Through the Twelve Steps*. He is also editor of *The Sexually Abused Male Volumes I & II*; *Child Survivors and Perpetrators of Sexual Abuse*; and *Adult Survivors of Sexual Abuse: Treatment Innovations*; and is co-author of *The First Step for People in Relationships with Sex Addicts*.

He has a master's degree in human development, a master's degree in education, and is currently working on a doctorate in clinical psychology.

Mic lives in St. Paul, Minnesota, with Kate An Greenbaum Hunter. His current photographic project is documenting a variety of regional vernacular folk art.

He wears a beard and gets his hair—at least what's left of it—cut in a barbershop, of course.